DRAG THE MAN DOWN

A CRIME NOVEL

GREGORY PAYETTE

DRAG THE MAN DOWN

For Mike and Lilly

Please Join My Reader List

I'd like to invite you to join my reader list to receive free stories, giveaways, and VIP announcements when my new books are released. When you do, you'll receive two free books, *Tell Them I'm Dead* and *What Have You Done?*

Visit **GregoryPayette.com/free-book** to sign up now.

1

GEORGE SISCO POURED himself a glass of beer from the pitcher and stared up at the TV on the back of the bar. The Sox were on late... a West Coast game against the Angels.

He turned to Roy and watched him as he looked around the bar.

In a hushed voice, Roy said, "I know you just got out and all but..." He paused a moment, looked around again. "You know Victor Albanese, don't you?"

"The boxer?"

Roy nodded. "Yeah. But now he's in the landscaping business."

George sipped his glass of beer and shrugged. "Why?"

"I don't know. Guess he likes landscaping."

George shook his head and rolled his eyes. "No, I mean why'd you ask if I know him?"

Roy looked back and forth along the bar and again leaned toward George. "I see him in Keenan's once in a while. He's been chirping about how much money he has... says he don't trust banks."

George glanced at Roy but didn't pay much attention at first.

"Victor was telling this guy I know that he keeps all his cash hidden in his house."

George sipped his beer, eyes up on the hockey game. He gave Roy a quick look out of the corner of his eye, but didn't say a word.

Roy slapped the back of his hand against George's arm. "Get this. He's out of town for a few days. And I know the guy who installed his alarm system in the house about fifteen years ago. Says he keeps trying to get Victor to replace it but he's too cheap."

George turned to Roy and shook his head. "Unh-uh. Don't even finish where you're going with this, Roy."

Roy shrugged. "You're the one who said you were broke. Frank pays you shit I bet, right? Same thing he paid you when you were fifteen? You can't even afford to fix that piece of shit car, right?"

George kept his eyes on the TV, grabbed a stale pretzel from the bowl in front of him and bit off a piece. He turned to Roy, and in a hushed voice so nobody else could hear him, he said, "I'm staying clean this time, Roy. I mean it."

George finished what was left in his glass, tossed a

couple dollars on the bar and stood from the stool. "Come on, I gotta get some sleep." He walked ahead of Roy and out the door.

Roy turned into the 7-Eleven parking lot from route 6. He shut off the ignition and glanced at George, "I know you said you don't want to hear it. But I'm telling you... we could both use a quick hit. We get lucky, maybe we come out of there with a few grand."

George stared out the windshield, toward the 7-Eleven. "Even if I wanted to, all you know is the guy said he's got money stashed in his house. But you have no idea where it is. Am I right? And the guy hasn't boxed in, what, ten years? Wouldn't be surprised he's broke, like the rest of us."

Roy shook his head. "I heard he's got a box with cash he built himself, attached to the bottom of his bed. Besides, he won a few titles in his day. And now he owns the landscaping business. I think he does alright."

George rubbed his face with both hands. He turned to Roy. "Sorry. I can't take the chance."

"But tonight might be our only chance. I don't know when he's coming back."

"You said he'd be away a few days."

Roy shrugged. "Might be. I'm just saying... strike

while the iron's hot, right?" He forced a smile, his eyebrows high on his forehead.

The door on the van cracked and popped as George pushed it open. He slid his hand in his pocket and jiggled the change as he walked toward the 7-Eleven.

Inside the store he opened the glass door on the back wall and reached in for a bottle of Gatorade. He walked to the counter and took a Three Musketeers candy bar from underneath. It reminded him of when he'd go with his father to see his old Aunt Nellie in the nursing home, with her pale face and long, white whiskers growing from her chin. She always kept a stash of Three Musketeers in the drawer next to her bed.

George paid the lady behind the counter with all the change he had from his pocket.

Roy was standing outside his van having a smoke when George walked out. Roy said, "I was thinking, how 'bout we take a ride by that house, check out the place? Maybe when you see it—it's a big house— you'll change your mind..."

George looked straight at Roy. "Jesus, Roy. What'd I say? I'm not going to do it. I'm different now. I'm a little older and—I'd like to think—a little wiser. I'm not saying I'm going straight forever... but I can't break into some guy's house because you overheard someone yapping about cash he won't put in a bank."

They both got back in the van.

George took a bite of his candy bar. He stared straight out the windshield as Roy backed out of the parking space. "You think I want to be mid-thirties like this, barely enough money to pay for a goddamn candy bar?" He shook his head in disgust. "Look at us, Roy."

"Hey, speak for yourself. I got my own business."

"Then why do you want to break into this guy's house? I heard you haven't had that much work."

Roy took a drag from his cigarette, burned down to the filter, and flicked it out the window. "It's seasonal, that's all."

George took another bite of his chocolate bar. "I just... I don't know. I did a lot of thinking while I was away. I might like to open my own place one day."

"Your own place? What's that mean?"

"A business. A restaurant. Maybe Pizza..something like Frank's."

Roy gave him a look with his eyebrows raised and half a smile on his face as he pulled out onto the street. "Are you serious?"

Roy drove the van into the neighborhood with the big houses built on large, wooded lots with long driveways. Some of the houses were lit up inside and out, bright like it was daylight. Others were dark with no sign of life inside. Although it *was* after midnight.

Roy said, "So how the hell are you going to open a restaurant when you make, what, nine bucks an hour working in a pizza place?"

George had his eyes out toward the houses, where all the rich people lived. It made him wish he had some kind of money. "I need to figure it out. Maybe I can borrow from the bank, get a small business loan."

Roy scratched the back of his head with his neck stretched over the steering wheel toward the windshield. He squinted his eyes. "Do you see any house numbers on those mailboxes?"

George didn't answer.

"You know, no bank's going to give a guy a loan who works in the back of a pizza place, gets paid under the table."

George kept quiet, his eyes on the big houses set far back from the street.

"You like those houses?" Roy said.

George glanced over at Roy. "Go fuck yourself, Roy."

"What the hell did *I* do?"

"You don't know when to shut up."

Roy pulled the car over and stopped in front of a dirt driveway. You could see floodlights through the trees, down at least a few hundred yards.

"That's it," Roy said with a nod toward the

driveway.

George stared out the passenger window. "I'm not doing it."

"What if... I don't know. What if we walk out of there... get lucky? You come out with a down payment on that restaurant."

George gave Roy a look. "Seriously, Roy. I gotta get home."

Roy backed the van up a few feet, turned the wheel and headed toward the house. "How about you wait in the car, I'll run in and be out in five minutes. I just want to look under that mattress."

George thought for a moment. "No, Roy. I'm not waiting out here for you."

Roy held his foot on the brake and leaned with his arms on the top of the steering wheel. He looked straight ahead toward the street. He shrugged. "Okay, can't say I didn't try." He slapped the van in reverse, backed up and turned in the other direction.

They drove away from Victor Albanese's house and neither spoke a word for the rest of the ride.

Roy pulled his van up in front of George's sister's house. "You happy?" he said. "Go ahead... hope you get a nice sleep on your sister's couch."

George pushed open the door, thanked Roy for the ride and slammed it closed. Something rattled underneath as George stood and watched Roy drive away, the right-rear tail light on the van blown out.

Joyce was still awake, out on the screened-in porch her ex-husband Louie'd converted to a three-season room when they were still married.

Joyce was George's sister.

She sat on the couch watching TV with a can of beer in her hand when George walked in. She turned to him and looked over her shoulder. "Where've you been?"

George stayed in the doorway. "My car wouldn't start."

She turned back towards the TV. "I told you not to buy that piece of shit."

George stepped back from the doorway and into the kitchen. He peeked into the other room with the couch where he'd been sleeping. He thought if Joyce wasn't always on the couch on the screened-in porch maybe he'd sleep out there, get some fresh air. But some nights Joyce never went to sleep at all.

"*George*," Joyce said with her loud, screechy voice.

He walked back out to the enclosed porch, looked at the back of her head. "What?"

"How'd you get home?"

"Roy."

She faced the TV and didn't turn to him. "You start hanging around with your loser friends again, you'll end up right back in the ACI."

2

GEORGE SAT OUTSIDE Bravos Coffee House in the courtyard of Founders Square in Providence. It was in the part of the city where you'd find locally owned restaurants and bakeries and coffee shops like the one where George sat and drank his coffee.

He didn't miss prison one bit. But as he looked around, he wasn't sure he missed Providence much, either. Other than Joyce, he didn't have much family around. His father died years before and his mother was long gone. She wasn't dead, just gone.

It was early September. The morning air was already cold as he sat alone at a small stone-like table in the cobblestone courtyard. He sipped his black coffee and thought about the night before. He wondered if he should've gone to Victor's house with Roy. He could've gotten out of there with something, at least so he didn't have to worry about paying for a decent cup of coffee.

There was no one else seated outside as George stared off at nothing in particular.

Something caught his eye. Some*one*, that is. His heart began to race as he finished his coffee. He got up from the table and walked out toward the street past the parked cars. He continued past the shops and the restaurants and the good smell that filled the air.

George was sure it was Dawn; the way she walked. He could see her confidence, even from a distance.

She turned a corner. George didn't want to lose her so he picked up his pace until he got close and saw her reach for the handle of Eva's Salon.

"*Dawn!*" he said with a little too much excitement just as she opened the door.

She stopped—the door just a few inches open—but she didn't turn around. Not right away.

"Dawn?" he said again.

After a brief pause she turned and looked over her shoulder. She let the door close. "George?" She stepped from the door and looked at him, her hands on her hips. "Are you following me?"

George shook his head. "No, I saw you from... I was having a coffee and—" His words felt garbled in his mouth. He cracked half a smile. "It's good to see you."

She narrowed her eyes. "I wish I could say the same, but..." She looked him up and down. "They let you out early?"

George didn't answer. "Are you getting a haircut?"

She gave him a look with a slight roll of her eyes. "No, they have good coffee."

George remembered why he could never get her out of his mind. It was more than because she was beautiful. He liked her attitude, her snappy bite where most people wouldn't know when she was being serious or not.

He didn't always know, either.

She pointed with her thumb behind her, toward the salon. "I gotta get back in there." She looked at her watch. "I'm late."

They stared into each other's eyes for a moment.

"Good to see you," he said.

She nodded, quiet for a couple of moments. "You already said that." She turned and opened the door to the salon and stepped inside.

George didn't move right away. He watched her sit down in the black chair in front of the window as she picked up a magazine.

She kept her head down, turning the pages.

He turned and walked away, then stopped and looked back at Dawn through the window. He saw her give him a look, then put her head back down before they made eye contact.

George had his bike that morning and rode it

through the streets, looking at some of the shops. There were a few with signs in the windows that said *For Lease*. One that caught his eye already had tables and chairs set up inside. It had a small bar toward the back. He got off his bike and leaned it against the corner of the brick building and walked up to the window. He looked inside with his hands on either side of his face to block the reflection from the sun.

There was a phone number on the sign, but right away he thought about what Roy had said, as if it was a secret:

'Who's going to give a man with a record and no job a loan to open a pizza joint?'

He got back on his bike and rode it over to Keenan's bar, even though it was still only eleven in the morning. He thought maybe his friend Jake was behind the bar, maybe'd hook him up with a drink or two.

He leaned his bike around the side and walked through the front door. Nobody was inside. Not Jake or any other bartender. George looked at his watch, glanced back at the door behind him, then went and sat down on a stool. He looked around at the empty tables. "Hello?"

The door at the back of the bar swung open. Jake walked through carrying five cases of beer between his thick, muscle-packed arms. He looked at George. "George? How long've you been out here?"

"Just walked in."

Jake didn't say much else, had his back to George as he leaned over and put the beers away in the cooler.

George said, "Any chance I can get a beer?"

Jake stopped what he was doing and straightened himself up to look at George. He paused a moment, wiping his hands on his smock. "Are you kidding?"

George stared back at him, a little caught off guard. He shrugged. "Why would I be kidding?" He looked at his watch. "Too early?"

Jake folded his arms at his chest. "You and Roy walked out on your tab the other night. Sixty-three dollars. Not including a tip."

"The other night?"

Jake turned around and stepped toward the register. He popped open the drawer and lifted the cash tray from inside. He pulled out a slip from underneath and put it down in front of George. He pointed down and smacked the paper with the tip of his finger.

George looked up at Jake. "We paid this tab. Didn't we? Why would I leave without paying?"

Jake leaned on the bar in front of George, his arms spread wide from his big shoulders with his sausage-like fingers wrapped around the edge of the bar. "If you paid your tab, I wouldn't be here saying you didn't."

"Roy paid you. I remember."

"You don't remember shit, the way you were

drinking," Jake said. "And when I asked Roy about it when you were leaving, he said *you* were paying. I looked up, you were already gone. Roy'd disappeared."

George slowly shook his head. "Jake, it's clearly a —"

"Pay the tab, I'll get you a beer."

George stood from the stool, reached into his pants and pulled out whatever money he had in his pocket. He slapped it down on the bar. "It's all I have. I'll pay you the rest later."

Jake counted out the money. "It's only fifty-six dollars."

George reached into his other pocket. He threw down a handful of coins and some lint. "I said I'll get you the rest. This is all I have."

Jake grabbed all the money—including the coins—and stuck it in the register. He took the slip from the bar, pulled the pen from behind his ear, and wrote down some numbers. "Five bucks, plus my tip, and we're good." He crumpled up the receipt and tossed it in the garbage. "I'll cover the rest." He leaned on the bar, again with his hands wide from his shoulders. "What'll you have?"

George stood quiet for a moment, cracked half a smile and shook his head. He looked Jake right in the eye, slapped his hand down on the bar and headed for the door. Over his shoulder, he said, "I'll bring you the rest tomorrow. Plus tip."

He left Keenan's and turned around the corner of the building for his bike. "Where the hell did I..."

It wasn't where he'd left it. He walked farther around the back of the building, wondering if he was losing his mind. He walked to the front of the building, looked back and forth along the sidewalk. "You gotta be shitting me," he said.

His bike had been stolen.

George didn't even have a phone. Not that he had anyone to call. But he didn't have a dime to his name, either. Not after he gave Jake his last penny. He wished he'd just walked out without paying Jake a thing.

It was at least a forty-five-minute walk back to his sister's house. Fifteen minutes on his bike, but that clearly wasn't an option.

He headed back to Founders Square where he'd been earlier for a coffee. Although he didn't know what good that would do since he had to get to work.

He walked along the street toward the salon where he last saw Dawn. And when he turned the corner, he saw her coming out the front entrance.

Her hair was short. Not short like a boy's haircut but shorter than you'd expect on a woman.

She looked good.

Dawn stopped as her eyes shifted toward George. She had a look on her face like she wanted to turn and go back inside or walk the other way and pretend she didn't see him. "Have you been waiting out here the whole time?" she said. There wasn't a hint of a smile on her face.

George shook his head. "Somebody stole my bike."

"Your bike? You still ride that thing everywhere?"

He shrugged. "Different bike." He hesitated a moment. "Any chance I could get a ride to Joyce's house?"

3

DAWN KEPT HER eyes on the road. She hadn't said much at all to George for the first few miles, but then gave him a quick glance. "I hope you know, this is a bit strange for me."

George looked back at her from the passenger seat "I wasn't sure if you were going to go the whole ride without talking, or..." He shrugged. "Of course it's weird. Last time I was in your car, you had me cuffed-up in the back seat."

Dawn reached down into the center console, pulled out a pair of sunglasses and slid them over her eyes.

George said, "I don't know why, but I thought you would've come out to visit me at some point."

"It's somewhat frowned upon in the department."

"To visit an ex-boyfriend in jail?" George kept his eyes on her. "I honestly hoped you felt bad about how it went down."

She turned and looked at him, shaking her head. "No, not at all." She gripped the wheel, twisting her hands on the wheel as if she was going to peel the leather right off.

George reached for the radio.

"What are you doing?" Dawn said.

"We can't listen to music? The silence is deafening."

He turned on an old Tom Petty song.

"Can you at least lower it?"

George rolled his eyes, reached forward and lowered the volume.

"So what are you doing for work?" she said. "I can't imagine it's easy finding a decent job after you get out..."

"No, it's not easy at all."

Dawn seemed to be a little more relaxed as the ride continued. "What about the restaurant? You still think about opening something?"

George shrugged. "Yeah, I think about it. That's about it though. Takes money. And I know it's not the most attractive thing to a woman... but I don't have much money."

Dawn stared straight ahead, quiet for a couple of moments. "George, I hope you don't think there's any chance of you and me—"

"No, not at all. Of course not." George forced out somewhat of a laugh. "Didn't even cross my mind." He turned and looked out the passenger window.

After another couple of miles without either one talking, Dawn stopped in front of Joyce's house. She shifted the car into park but left it running. She looked out toward the house.

George opened the car door and put one foot outside. He turned back to Dawn. "I appreciate the ride." He kept his gaze on her as he waited for her to turn his way. "If there's a chance you and I can grab a coffee one morning, maybe—"

Dawn turned, pulled her sunglasses down off her face as she stared back at him and shook her head. "No, George. I'm sorry."

He kept his eyes on hers for a moment, then stepped out of the car. "Appreciate the ride," he said as he slammed the door closed behind him.

George was in the kitchen at Frank's Pizza with his head in the refrigerator. He removed a boiled ham when his sister's ex-husband, Louie, walked in the back door.

"Hey Louie." George lifted the five-pound ham up onto the slicer. He walked to the sink and washed his hands, wiped them on his stained, white smock and shook Louie's hand.

"Frank around?" Louie said. He looked toward the dining area out front.

George shook his head. "He went to the bank."

He turned on the slicer. "You need him?"

Louie waited a moment, leaned his back up against the stainless steel table next to George.

George slid his arm back-and-forth on the meat slicer like he was using a handsaw. He held his hand underneath to catch each slice of ham, flipped each slice and placed it in a neat pile.

"I talked to Joyce," Louie said. "She said your car shit the bed, you can't afford to fix it?"

"I shouldn't have bought it. But, no, I can't fix it. Probably not worth it, anyway." He focused on the ham for a moment, slipped a piece in his mouth and said, "I picked up a bike for sixty bucks, but someone stole it."

Louie folded his arms and looked down toward the floor. "I know Frank doesn't pay you shit. I thought maybe you'd be interested in doing a little something on the side."

George slid his arm back and forth, catching each slice of ham as it dropped from the slicer. "I don't know what you have in mind. But Roy already tried to get me to break into someone's house." He slapped the button on the slicer and turned it off. "I'm fresh out of the can, Louie, so I'm not about to take any chances."

"What'd you, come out a changed man?"

George shrugged. "Prison can do that to you."

"What if there's an opportunity, you won't have to worry about working in a place like this, slicing pig in the back of a pizza place?"

"If it's not something on the up-and-up, then—"

"It depends how you want to look at it," Louie said.

George filled the clear, plastic fish-bucket with all five pounds of ham and squeezed the cover over the top.

The back door opened and Frank walked through carrying a cardboard box of tomatoes. "Look who it is," he said with a nod toward Louie. "If I knew you'd be in here I would've locked my office."

George sprayed down the slicer, leaned over it and wiped it clean.

Frank looked at Louie. "Can't you see the man's trying to work?" He placed the box of tomatoes next to the slicer in front of George. "Cut these up next, will you? We're almost out, hopefully they'll get us through lunch."

Louie said under his breath, "Slave labor." He turned and walked toward the back door.

"*What's that?*" Frank said as he turned to Louie.

"Pay the guy a decent wage... he could at least fix his car. The prices you charge, you could at least afford to pay your help a little more."

"I don't remember the last time I saw you in here, spending all that money you supposedly make."

Louie reached for the door. "George, we'll catch up later." He turned from the doorway with the door open and glanced at George. "You need a ride home tonight?"

George shook his head. "Thanks, but Roy said he'd come by."

George stood at the front of the restaurant, looked at his watch and wondered if Roy forgot he needed a ride. He turned and looked through the windows of the restaurant. Frank was still inside closing up as he walked around inside. He turned off the lights.

George wasn't in the mood for talking to Frank so he walked around the back of the building. He waited for Roy by his broken-down car parked next to the dumpster

Frank drove around from the other side in his sixty-seven Corvette. It had PIZZA on the license plate. He looked like he was about to pull out onto the street, but must've noticed George. His reverse lights kicked on, he backed up and leaned over to crank down the passenger side window. "Are you going to get that piece of junk out of here? Can't have this place looking like a salvage yard."

George nodded. "Yeah, I'll get it towed tomorrow."

"You said that yesterday."

"Don't worry, I will."

Frank gave George a nod. "You need a ride?"

George looked past the Corvette toward the road. "Roy should be on his way."

"Okay, have a good night, George." Frank squealed his tires as he took off, the 'Vette roared as the back end fishtailed out onto the street.

4

GEORGE SAT IN the dark on the three-season porch, the only light—other than the moonlight from outside—came from the red bulb on the cable box under the TV. He had a can of Coors Light he took from the refrigerator.

Joyce was already in bed.

He sat on the couch, tired after the long walk from Frank's Pizza. It took well over an hour.

He wondered what happened to Roy. It wasn't like him. If Roy said he'd give you a ride, he'd be there.

But George thought maybe Roy was still upset George didn't want to break into Victor's house. He didn't bother calling Roy, either... just figured he'd check in with him in the morning.

George thought about prison. He thought about how there was always someone around. It wasn't like he liked the other prisoners. But he found it interesting. The whole social structure.

He'd read a lot of books on the inside, but hadn't cracked a single page since he'd gotten out. In some ways, he thought, you didn't have much to worry about behind bars. Other than, well, getting your ass kicked or being gang raped.

But other than that...

George sipped from the can of Coors Light, held it up in front of him and wondered why Joyce drank the stuff. He could drink a twelve pack and not feel a thing. He thought about what Louie'd said, what he had in mind to make some extra money or—as Louie put it—*money on the side*.

Joyce's house *used* to belong to Louie. It was his before he married Joyce. Then they got divorced and Joyce got the house. Louie ended up in a three-decker on the wrong side of town.

It was Joyce who cheated on Louie, but he jumped at the chance to bail. He even gave her the house, no argument.

Depending on what Louie had in mind, George couldn't see himself working for Louie. They'd done some jobs together, but it was whenever George would bring Louie in, not the other way around.

George finished the can of beer and reached for the remote. He turned on the TV and it was already on the channel Joyce'd always watch: another real estate show with some young, cocky kid with his hair slicked back... his hot wife swinging a hammer in the background.

George pointed the remote at the TV with one eye closed, like he was sighting a rifle, made a noise with his mouth like he'd shot the punk on the TV.

He turned the TV off and tossed the remote on the cushion next to him. He leaned forward on the couch with his elbows resting on his knees, his hands folded together in front of him. He wondered if it was even possible to make a living on the straight side of the line... the one he'd crossed hundreds of times ever since he was old enough to know better.

He'd mostly robbed houses, but when he learned how to crack a safe... that's when he started to make real money.

He'd stolen from jewelry stores once in a while, too. One time he stole a high-priced piece of art from a gallery up in Boston. He got to a point where he could score ten, twenty, thirty grand without a problem.

He leaned and turned on the lamp next to the couch, got up and grabbed a glass from the dry bar and poured himself a Jim Beam. He threw it back. Then had another. And another until he walked back to the couch and sat down with the bottle in one hand, his glass in the other.

He drank until they both were empty.

When he got up, it took a moment for him to get his footing. He walked through the doorway and into the room where he slept on the couch. He pulled out a pair of dark jeans and threw a dark sweatshirt on over his head. He picked up his duffle bag, dumped his clothes on the couch and threw the empty duffle bag over his shoulder.

Out in the kitchen he grabbed Joyce's keys from the hook by the door. He walked through one of the doorways and into the garage where he reached for the pegboard and pulled down a pry bar.

George walked out the back door of the garage and around front stepped into Joyce's maroon Buick. He tried to be quiet as he pulled the door closed. Last thing he wanted to do was wake Joyce.

He started the car, turned on the radio and turned up the volume. David Bowie played as he backed out of the driveway. He slapped the top of the steering wheel to the beat of the music and smiled as he pulled out onto route 6. He drove a couple of miles, keeping at the speed limit.

He turned down Dawson Lane, toward the neighborhoods with all the big houses. He never liked rich people, and made it a point—whenever he'd break into a home—to not take from someone who couldn't afford to have things stolen. People with too much money, he felt, had too much stuff to begin with.

He recognized Victor's driveway right away, the way the lights lit up around the house. It was at least a hundred yards from the road. He turned the Buick down the driveway and drove toward the house.

George walked around the house and looked through every window on the first floor. Roy had said the alarm system was old, so he knew it wouldn't be much of a problem.

He cracked the bottom of a window with the pry bar he took from Joyce's garage, ready to run if the alarm went off.

But it didn't.

It'd been a while. He wasn't the least bit nervous as he slipped the ski mask over his face, just in case there were cameras inside. The mask felt itchy and made him sweat. It was hard to concentrate as he scratched the side of his face.

George was always prepared. But, for one reason or another, he only broke into houses when he was drunk. He'd even made a name for himself. Dawn had once said they called him 'Jim Beam' at the station. But he didn't know if she was serious.

He pushed open the window and crawled inside.

The house was big and wide-open. The walls seemed to go on forever, mostly covered with framed photos of Victor Albanese standing in the ring.

George never really followed boxing, and didn't know much about Victor other than he'd won some fights. But as he looked at the pictures with the large crowds in the background and the belts Victor held high over his head, he knew Victor had more success than he'd realized.

He moved his flashlight inside the dark house, along the walls. A large, square display case with a wood frame and a glass-like front hung on the wall. It was filled with trophies and a handful of rings on small shelves. In the middle of the display was a gold-colored belt, laced with what looked like emeralds. George had no idea if they were real.

He reached inside his duffle bag and removed the pry bar. Rather than smash the glass, he slipped it into the side of the frame and pushed. He tried to break the whole thing from the wall, but instead put a crack along the frame. He pushed again, but it wouldn't budge.

Rather than waste any more time, he took the steel pry bar and smashed the glass. Shards of glass covered the belt and the shelves inside.

He grabbed the belt and the handful of rings and stuffed them into his bag. He didn't take the trophies.

George looked at his watch, the timer running. It'd been three minutes.

He thought for a moment, looked toward the stairs and ran up to the second floor with his long legs stretched as he skipped every other step. He stood at the top of the stairs and looked back and forth.

The first room he looked inside was a pink room

with shelves filled with dolls and toys. He stepped back out into the hall and hurried toward the far end of the hall and into a large, master bedroom.

The bed inside was bigger than any George had seen, even in all the other big homes he'd broken into. He pulled the black comforter off, ripped off the sheets, and strained as he lifted the mattress. It must've weighed at least two hundred pounds.

There was nothing underneath between the mattress and the box spring. It wasn't much of a surprise, but he'd seen enough times where people kept a lot of money and valuable possessions under a mattress.

Dumb rich people.

"Shit," he said as he turned and scanned the room. With his foot he pushed on the box spring from the bed. The box Roy had mentioned was bolted to the bottom of the metal frame. George reached for his bag and used his pry bar to break it free. The box crashed to the floor.

Sweat had soaked through the ski mask. He lifted it from his face and ran his sleeve along his mouth. He didn't think there'd be cameras in the bedroom. He hoped not, anyway.

The box had a lock on it but with one swing of the pry bar he had it open. Just as Roy had said, there was plenty of cash inside. All hundreds... Benjamins. He closed the lid and stuck the box under one arm and threw his duffle bag over the other.

He ran for the door and as soon as he stepped outside, he saw blue lights flashing down toward the street. It was far enough away, still out on the street. They didn't seem to be in the driveway.

George tried to stay calm, thought for a second about running into the woods. But he knew he'd made a mistake. He should've never taken Joyce's car up the driveway. Maybe, he thought, he could hide her car in the woods around the back of the house.

Sure enough, headlights turned up the driveway. Still over a hundred yards away, but moved toward him.

He turned and ran back into the house, through the kitchen and reached for the door he hoped was the garage.

It was. Without turning on the lights, he felt around for the garage door opener. He hit the first button he felt and the door began to open. The light on the ceiling came on automatically. George looked along the wall and grabbed a spade shovel. He swung it over his head and hit the light. The smashed bulb shattered and glass fell onto his head and down to the floor.

He ran from the garage and jumped into Joyce's car, killing the interior light; careful not to tap the brakes. He started the engine and jammed it into drive, drove straight into the garage without tapping the brakes. He killed the engine but drove into the back wall. The car stopped right there and he jumped out to close the door.

George crouched down below a window and peeked up over the sill. The blue lights from the cop's car moved up the driveway. A spotlight casted a long, bright light around the yard. The light moved back and forth toward the woods along the yard and reflected off the trees.

He stayed low on the damp concrete floor, his back pressed against the wall as a light shined in the windows and bounced around the interior of the garage. He could hear his own heavy breathing inside himself as he tried to control each breath. But it only made it harder to breath.

A car door slammed outside. Lights again came through the garage windows, but then everything went dark. He heard the car door slam shut.

George stayed in a crouched position but turned and peeked out through the lower part of the window. He watched as the blue lights turned off and the car's rear tail lights began to fade. The cop's car turned and drove away from Victor's house.

But then the red brake lights came on. The cop had stopped and didn't move for a moment. George waited, his eyes on the brake lights out in the road. Then the car began to move and he watched to make sure the cop was gone.

5

GEORGE WOKE UP on the couch and heard Joyce talking to someone outside with her usual, loud voice. He grabbed his watch from the floor and saw it wasn't even nine in the morning.

He pulled the curtain back and looked out toward the driveway. Roy was outside with his van. He was talking to Joyce.

George walked to the front door and went outside, gave Roy a nod but didn't even look at Joyce. "What's going on?"

"Hey, George," Roy said. "I need to apologize for not showing up last night. I wish you'd get a phone... I would've called. I called Frank's... nobody answered."

George nodded. "We must've been closed."

Joyce had her hands on her hips and turned toward her car. She said to George, "Did you use my car last night?"

George stared back at her for a moment before he answered. "Uh... Hope it's okay. I didn't want to wake you, but something came up and—"

"At three in the morning?"

Roy watched as he looked off for a moment.

"The only reason anyone would go out at three in the morning, is if they're up to something." She looked at Roy, her arms still folded at her chest. "Am I right?"

Roy shrugged and turned to George. "Where'd you go?" He cracked a smile, his eyebrows high up on his head. "You out, trying to get laid?"

Joyce gave Roy a look and knocked the smile off his face without having to raise a finger.

George looked right at Joyce "I would've asked, but didn't want to wake you."

"I hope you at least put gas in it. I gotta work... don't have time to—"

"I'll fill it up next time," he said.

Joyce kept a stare on George, stone-faced, slowly shook her head and walked back inside.

George rubbed his face up and down with both hands, rubbed the back of his neck and left his hand there.

"What *were* you doing at three in the morning?" Roy said.

"It was nothing."

Of course, George wasn't about to tell Roy what he was doing, especially since it was Roy who told him about Victor Albanese's house in the first place. Even if George offered to split the cash he took from the box or whatever he'd get for the belt, it wouldn't go over well with Roy. He took everything personal.

George tried to change the subject, "You know where I can get a cheap phone? Something I can use when I'm looking for a ride?"

Roy said, "I told you I was sorry."

George smiled. "I just need a phone for emergencies. But I would only give the number to certain people."

"You need a burner phone?"

George shrugged. "I guess." He said, "Can you give me a ride, go get a phone? I'll take you out to breakfast... my treat."

"You have money all of a sudden?"

George nodded. "Enough for breakfast. And a phone."

George and Roy sat at a small table in the middle of Zip's Diner in Pawtucket. George played with his new phone. "I don't know how I feel about having a phone, like I'm always within reach."

"You had one before, didn't you?"

George nodded. "I didn't like it then, either."

"You'd rather have to drive around, look for a

payphone?"

"Wasn't that bad, was it? You only made a call when you had a good reason. Now everyone's on their phones."

Roy paused for a couple of moments. "So what's your new number?"

George was about to tell him, but the waitress came up to their table with two coffees. "Good morning," she said. She glanced at George. "Have I seen you in here before?"

He stared at her and took a moment before he answered. "I don't know. I haven't been around in a while."

She cracked a slight smile without taking her eyes off his. "Well, you look familiar. I just—"

"Small state I guess, right?"

She nodded with a shrug. "I guess."

They ordered their food and George watched her walk away. He liked her look, even in her silly diner uniform like she came out of the fifties... the way her long legs came out from under her skirt.

"Jesus Christ," Roy said. "I've had my eyes on her for six months, leave good tips, try to be nice... she still doesn't know who I am. You're in here five minutes, she's ready to jump in your pants."

George sipped his coffee, looked at Roy over the rim of his cup. "I don't think she meant anything by it," he said. "She thought she knew me... nothing more to it." He leaned his head down and lowered his voice. "Maybe she saw my mugshot on the news."

The waitress was out with their food, re-filled their cups with the pot of coffee then smiled at George. "Anything else?"

George shook his head and smiled back. "No, thank you." He took a bite of his toast and looked around the place. "A lot of old people in here."

Roy had his head down and shoveled fried eggs in his mouth like he hadn't had a bite to eat in days. Yellow yoke dripped off the corner of his mouth as he looked up at George. "Huh?"

George stared back at him but didn't bother to repeat himself. "Guess who I saw the other day."

Roy shrugged and shook his head, his mouth too full to talk.

George waited to answer, like he wanted to build the suspense. "Dawn."

Roy swallowed hard to get it all down and wiped the corner of his mouth with his napkin. "No shit?"

"I was downtown, getting a coffee at Bravos. She was getting a haircut."

"Does she still look good?"

George nodded as he sipped his coffee. "Yeah, of course she does. She has short hair now."

"You talk to her?"

George dipped his toast in his runny yoke and took a bite as he nodded. "She gave me a ride home. She wasn't too excited about it, though."

"What do you expect? She's a cop. Not to mention, the one who put you in the can."

The pretty waitress came back to their table and poured coffee in both their cups without asking. She glanced at George.

He looked at her chest, her shirt button down low in the front. But he was only trying to read her name tag. "Kim? This here is my friend, Roy. He comes in here a lot more than I do, and I'm sure he'd be afraid to tell you this himself... but he has a crush on you." George smiled as her face turned red.

But not as red as Roy's face... so red it looked like it was going to blow.

Roy had a nervous look to his face and did nothing, other than giving her a nod.

"I'm George, by the way."

She pointed at the name tag on her chest. "This isn't mine. My name's Sam. I forgot my name tag at home, thought I'd have a little fun... especially with the old men who come in here and stare at my chest."

"I didn't think you looked like a *Kim*," George said.

"Do I look like a *Sam*?"

George's eyes caught an old man with a cook's hat on his head as he watched them through the kitchen window. "That guy looks like a Sam."

She turned and laughed. "It's Samantha. My friends call me Sam."

George nodded. "Good to meet you, Samantha."

She kept her eyes on George for a moment. "You, too." She turned to Roy. "Both of you."

Roy turned in his seat and they both stared as she walked away.

George sipped his coffee, smiled behind the cup as he took a sip and looked at Roy. "Hey, I stopped by Keenan's for a beer. Jake was behind the bar, all pissed off... said we walked out on our tab." George looked past Roy, caught Samantha looking his way, but she turned as soon as they made eye contact.

Roy followed George's eyes, but Samantha had already disappeared. "What're you looking at?"

"Nothing. I was just saying, Jake was pissed. Made me pay him sixty bucks from the other night."

Roy shook his head. "We didn't stiff him." He paused a moment. "Did we?"

George thought for a moment. "Doesn't matter, we're square. I paid him what I could. He's kind of an asshole anyway."

Roy leaned over the table, closer to George. In a hushed voice, he said, "Jake's the one who told me about Victor Albanese." He looked back and forth, his voice in almost a whisper. "I still think we oughta take a shot at it, George. Can be in and out of there in—"

George wiped his mouth and folded his napkin, tucked it under his dish. "I gotta get to work," George said before Roy could even say anything else. He grabbed the bill and got up from his seat, pulled a twenty from his pocket and threw it on the table.

"You're leaving a twenty-dollar tip?" Roy said.

George didn't answer, walked to the front and paid the old lady behind the register.

6

GEORGE CALLED JOYCE at work. When she answered, all she said was *"What,"* but not at all like she was asking a question.

"Jesus," George said. "Do you have to sound so pleasant at work?"

"I'm busy. And you left me with hardly any gas."

George said, "There was at least half a tank. I only drove a few miles."

After a brief pause, she said, "What do you want? An old man just died, I have to clean out the room, get it ready so we can get someone else in here."

"Can I have Louie's number?"

"For what?"

"What do you mean *for what?* I need to call him."

"Don't you have it?" she said.

George closed his eyes with the phone up to his ear and took a deep breath. "If I had it, Joyce, I wouldn't have called you."

"What do you have to hang around with my ex-husband for anyway?"

George was tempted to hang up the phone as he held it away from his ear, looked at the screen. "He said something about a job."

"Yeah, I'm sure it's a real reputable position. You need to be careful... you'll end up right back in the can."

George thought for a moment. "Can I just have his number?"

"When do you want to meet?" Louie said to George when he called.

"I have to work at two," George said.

"Well, maybe after we talk you won't need to go in."

"I wouldn't do that to Frank." George paused for a moment. "Where are we meeting?"

"Meet me at Keenan's," Louie said.

"I'd rather go somewhere else. What about Zip's Diner?"

"No, I'd like a cocktail. Just meet me at Keenan's in an hour, stop being so difficult." Louie hung up.

George had picked up a bike earlier in the day— got it used from Craigslist for eighty bucks. He rode it all the way to Keenan's and stood outside. He heard his name.

"George." It was Louie, walking toward him along the sidewalk. He looked down at George's bicycle. "What the hell's this?"

George knew where Louie was going but played along. "What's what?"

"Why're you riding a bicycle?"

George shrugged. "What's wrong with riding a bike?"

"A bike? A Harley's a *bike*. This is a bicycle." He looked up at George. "No basket with it?" He laughed as he shook his head and walked in the front door of Keenan's.

George followed behind him, pushed his bike through the doorway with his foot against the bottom of the door to hold it open.

He looked up and saw Jake behind the bar, watching him. "What the hell are you doing?" Jake had his hands on his hips.

George stopped. "I thought we were square?"

"I'm talking about the bike. You can't bring that in here."

The place was empty, except for Louie... already with a drink in his hand. He turned in the stool as he took a sip from his glass, looking back and forth from Jake to George.

"My bike got stolen out here yesterday."

"And how is that my problem?" Jake said.

George stood by the door, holding the bike. "I didn't say it was. But I don't need this one getting ripped off."

Jake looked at Louie. "Why's he riding a bike?"

Louie shrugged. "That's what I asked him."

George turned around with the bike, ready to walk out the door. He wasn't going to say another word... wished he'd never walked in.

Louie stood from the barstool. "Where you goin'?"

George stopped and turned.

Louie gave Jake a look. "What's it matter, he has his bike in here? The place is empty."

Jake shrugged a shoulder as Louie walked over to George and grabbed the bike, leaned it against the wall next to the door. He put his arm around George's shoulders and walked him toward the back of the bar. "Come on, let's talk business."

George sat down at a table as Louie walked over to the bar, grabbed a beer for George and got himself a Jim Beam. He sat down at the table across from George. He said, "You're getting a little sensitive. You used to be able to take a little ribbing." He narrowed his eyes, dropped his eyebrows low. "Hope you didn't act like that in prison... sensitive ones get it in the pokie."

George sipped from the bottle of beer, stared back at Louie without saying a word. He looked at his watch. "I don't have a lot of time... unless you can give me a ride to work."

Louie shrugged. "Relax... finish your drink. I'll give

you a ride." He looked back and forth and over at the bar, made sure Jake—who was always a little nosey—wasn't paying attention. "Hey, so you know who Victor Albanese is?"

George was about to sip his beer but stopped, put it back down on the table. "You serious?"

Louie nodded. "Yeah, I'm serious. Why, you know him?"

George hesitated a moment, couldn't help but think Roy put Louie up to it. But he didn't bring up Roy's name. "I know of him. Owns a landscaping place."

Louie said, "Before that, he was a pretty good fighter." Again, Louie looked over his shoulder toward Jake, turned back to George. "Guy comes in here all the time, brags about all the fights he won... how he kicked this one's ass... knocked this one out."

George thought about the belt, wasn't about to say a word about it to Louie.

Louie said, "So he tells everyone he's going out of town, out of the country... somewhere in Europe. Italy or something, see his family."

George said, "Isn't he Albanian?"

Louie shrugged. "I dunno. Italian, I thought." He pulled his chair in closer to the table, leaned toward George. He looked over his shoulder, then back at George. "He's got championship belts on display at his house. Heard they're secured but... what I hear, they're worth a couple hundred thousand a piece."

George swallowed hard as he tried to keep his face straight. "How many belts does he have?"

"Guy won three championships." Louie's face got twisted. "You didn't know that?"

George shrugged a shoulder as he sipped his beer. "I never paid much attention."

"Then you never sat next to him at the bar. Guy'll chew your ear off, tell you every goddamn detail about every fight, like anybody gives a shit." Louie shook his head, sipped his Jim Beam. "Don't get me wrong, gotta respect the guy. But, come on, how many times I gotta hear the same story."

"I guess I know where you're going with all this, Louie. And like I already told you, I'm done with—"

"Will you just let me finish? Hear me out?"

George wasn't even listening, his mind spinning as he thought about the belt he already took from Victor's house and hid in his sister's garage. He had no idea if that was worth what Louie'd said. He didn't know and didn't ask if Louie and Roy were in this together. Although Roy only mentioned the cash, never said a word about the belts.

"How do you know the belts are worth that much money?"

Louie said, "Victor said it himself, like I said, braggin' about everything. Guy's a real loud mouth. But I asked around—just curious, you know?— thinking maybe he was full of shit. Even called the IBF, talked to some broad, but she didn't seem to know shit."

"IBF?"

"International Boxing Federation." Louie sipped his Jim Beam. "She puts me through to this guy, starts asking me a bunch of questions, like it's a fucking interrogation. I hung up."

"So you don't know?"

"I called another guy I know. A collector... deals in sports memorabilia, baseball cards, signed photographs, stuff like that. Tells me one of 'em could be worth half-a-million, if it was the belt he had in mind... loaded up with diamonds and emeralds. The belt itself, part of it might be made of alligator skin."

George's heart pounded in his chest, the adrenaline made it hard for him to sit still. He thought he'd been lucky, got a boxing belt that'd maybe fetch him a couple grand. But now with Louie telling him another story...

He kept his mouth shut, but knew he'd need Louie's help. Louie was the man who could turn anything into cash. A championship belt wasn't something you'd sell on eBay, or meet some guy in a parking lot from Craigslist.

"So whaddya think?" Louie said. "You interested?"

7

GEORGE GOT OFF work late and rode his bike to Joyce's house. He knew he'd need to do a much better job of hiding the belt he'd stolen from Victor. That's all he needed, he thought... Joyce wakes up with a hair across her ass, starts cleaning out the garage.

A good mile from Joyce's house, bright headlights came up behind him from a police vehicle that seemed to slow... then drove right by him. He couldn't see inside but watched as it passed.

The brake lights came on as the car stopped.

George got closer and rode up on the grass as he tried to go around it and took a quick glance through the driver's side window.

It was Dawn.

He stopped. "I hope you're not out looking for me," he said, mostly joking but you never know.

She put down her window and looked down at his

bike. "You found it?"

George wasn't sure what she meant at first. "Oh, the bike?" He shook his head. "This is a different one." He forced a smile but felt like a dope out in the dark, in the middle of the night, on his bike.

She nodded with her lips pressed together as she turned from him and she looked toward the front of her car. Her hand hung limp with her wrist resting on the top of the steering wheel.

George liked how she looked in uniform. He always did... except for when she had to arrest him.

"You know, I was going to ask around for it," she said.

He stared at her with a blank look on his face.

"Your bike... the one you said was stolen? But you'd need to file a report, report it missing."

George nodded. "I know how it works."

She stared back at him for a moment, then moved the shifter on the column. The lights on the rear of her car brightened. She said, "Be careful out there." The car moved forward as she put up her window.

"You too," he said as she drove away. He stood and watched the car until it turned the corner and disappeared.

His phone vibrated in his pocket just as he started to pedal. He hated having the damn phone, as if there was ever anyone in his life he had to hear from. He couldn't think of anyone. Dawn, maybe... but that ship had sailed.

He answered anyway. "Hello?"

"Look at that, you answered it."

"Hey Roy, what's up?"

"I just left Keenan's. Jake said you were in there earlier with Louie."

George said, "I hope you gave him the tip you owed him."

"What tip?"

"The tip from the other night... he said we stiffed him, remember?"

Roy was quiet for a moment. "He's gotten enough tips from me over the years."

"I gotta get moving, Roy. Did you want something?"

"What's wrong with *you*?" Roy said.

"What's wrong with me? Nothing at all. I'm on my bike... I just want to get home."

"I was just wondering... what Louie talked to you about?"

George looked at the screen of his phone, tempted to toss it in the woods and forget about it. "Are you *serious*?" George said.

"Serious about *what*?"

"You're really asking me what Louie and I were doing?"

"I didn't ask what you were doing. Was just wondering what you were talking about."

George took a deep breath and shook his head, the phone still up against his ear. "Roy, can we talk later? I really want to get home."

"Was it about Victor Albanese?"

George went quiet, still unsure if both Roy and Louie were in this together or if they'd even discussed any of it. But it seemed like they both coincidentally approached George about the same thing. Nothing more to it. Louie'd been the one who mentioned the belts. "Victor Albanese? No, never said a word about him."

Roy was quiet for a moment.

George pulled himself off his bike and walked along the dark street.

"Don't lie to me, George. Okay? I've known you a hell of a lot longer than Louie has. And I hope you know you don't have to—"

"Jesus Christ, Roy. I wish you'd just come right out and ask me what you want to know."

"You don't have to be like that with me, George. I was just..."

The two were quiet, and George was in no mood to deal with Roy. "Let's talk tomorrow." George hung up the phone and stuck it back in his pocket. He hopped up on his bike and started to ride. He wondered why he came back at all... how he thought maybe he would've been better off if he'd headed south or west when he got out of prison... why the hell'd he stay in Rhode Island?

As he turned at a pretty good speed into the driveway, he hit his brakes and cut off onto the grass. He had to avoid Joyce's car in the driveway.

He didn't know why she wasn't still at work.

The garage door was open wide. He got off his bike, walked past Joyce's car and went into the garage. His eyes shot to the box on the shelf where he'd stuffed the belt and the cash he took from Victor's.

He walked the bike inside the garage and leaned it up against the back wall.

The door to the house that opened to the breezeway opened. Joyce stuck her head outside. *"What the hell are you doing?"* she said.

"Nothing. Putting my bike away."

She looked down at the bike. "You got a new bike?"

George didn't answer as Joyce stared back at him.

"Why's the garage door open," he said.

She stepped down into the garage. "It wasn't open when I got home."

"When did you get home?" he said.

She looked at her watch and shrugged. "I don't know. An hour ago?"

"And you didn't open it?"

She just shook her head and walked past him, out toward the driveway. He stood quiet as she looked around her car. "You think someone was in here?"

George's heart raced. He wanted her to go back inside so he could look in the box... make sure the belt and cash weren't gone. For some reason he'd lost his knack for staying cool. He felt anxious ever since he walked out of those prison gates. "Doesn't look like anything's missing," he said, trying to coax her back inside.

She gave him a look. "How would you know if something was missing?"

He shrugged. "I'm just saying, why would someone come here, open the garage?" He looked around and nodded toward the driveway. "Your car's right there."

She stepped back in the garage and walked past him. "Did you ever break into a house when someone was home?"

He didn't answer, just said, "I'm sure it's nothing."

A slight breeze could be felt from outside as the door at the back of the garage opened.

They both exchanged a look

"That door should be locked," she said.

George walked toward the door and stepped outside into the back yard. He looked around but didn't see a thing. The only light came from the TV in the three-season room off the back of the house

Joyce stood in the doorway behind him, still inside the garage. "I should call the cops."

George's head snapped around. "It's nothing to worry about, Joyce. You're being paranoid."

"Don't tell me I'm being paranoid. Someone must've been in here."

"Joyce, if it was someone looking for something...

they're long gone. Maybe you hit the button on the garage door opener by accident when you got home."

She folded her arms at her chest and shook her head. "No, I didn't."

8

GEORGE WAS IN the mood for diner food and took his bike over to Zip's. Of course, he'd hoped he might bump into Samantha, the pretty waitress he'd met with Roy. He had no way of knowing if she'd be there or if she'd remember him, although he had no real plans of making any moves anyway. He just wanted to see her.

Inside the diner was quiet, with plenty of open tables and a few stools at the counter. He sat at a table at the end, under a window, and opened the paperback he brought with him.

George liked to read. He must've gone through at least a hundred books in prison, but hadn't picked one up since he got out. When he was a kid, his grandmother would take him to the library and read to him a lot when he was younger.

He was glad she wasn't around to see how he'd turned out.

It was another one of the inmates, an older gentleman, who'd turned him on to reading again. He once told George, "The best novelists teach you more about the world than you'll ever get from the newspaper."

George's nerves boiled in his stomach as he looked around for Samantha. But the only waitress he saw was the gray-haired older woman who looked his way. He remembered her from behind the cash register when he was there with Roy.

She put her finger up toward George, telling him to wait, as she poured coffee for three old men who sat elbow-to-elbow at the counter in front of her.

George took a quick look at the menu, not really focused on what was in it. He closed it and cracked open the book he picked up at the used bookstore a couple of blocks away.

The old-lady waitress stopped at his table. "Sorry for the wait," she said. She held her small notepad up in front of her, the pen rested on the paper. "You know what you'd like, hon?"

When he looked up at her, he saw her eyes were going out the window, toward the parking lot.

He took a look himself, and saw Samantha standing out by the sidewalk. She had a backpack over her shoulder. There was a bus sign over her head and he assumed she was leaving.

George jumped from his seat. "Sorry, I just remembered something... I mean, I forgot something outside." He headed for the door—the old lady watched him, not saying a word—and left the diner.

He walked up to Samantha out by the street. "Samantha?"

She looked at him, her head tilted but she didn't say anything at first.

"It's George. I was here the other day... with my friend Roy."

A smile filled her face. "Oh, yes. Of course. I knew it was you, I guess I was just—" She looked toward the diner and the empty parking lot. "What are you doing here?"

He pointed back toward the diner with his thumb. "I came by to get something to eat. Isn't that what most people come here for?" He smiled, letting her know he wasn't being a jerk, although it could've come out that way.

"I'm sorry, I meant, uh... I'm just waiting for a ride."

George nodded toward his bike. "I'd offer you a ride, but..."

She let out a slight laugh. "Thanks anyway." Sam turned back toward the street, her eyes on the cars speeding by. "He should be here any minute." She pulled out her phone and looked at the screen, then toward the oncoming cars.

"Okay, well... it was nice seeing you again," he said as he took a few steps backward, toward his bike. "I should head home now anyway, before it gets too dark to ride." He turned and walked away from her.

She said, "It's George, right?"

He turned his head and over his shoulder said, "Yes... Sam."

"I thought you came here to eat?"

He stopped and walked back to her. "You know, I was just thinking... maybe—I don't know—we could grab a coffee one morning?"

An engine roared and tires squealed as a newer model Dodge Charger pulled up to the curb in front of Sam. The kid behind the wheel—at least he looked like a kid to George—revved the engine and stared out toward George... gave him a look.

Sam opened the passenger door and glanced back at George as she stepped inside the car.

She hadn't answered his question.

The strong smell of cologne seeped out from the car as the kid with the slicked-back hair looked past Sam at George. George heard him say, "Who's that?"

"A customer," she said as she strapped the seatbelt across her body and slammed the door closed.

George stood and watched, his eyes locked with the kid who—he'd guessed—must've been Samantha's boyfriend.

The Charger took off. The tires squealed and the smell of burnt rubber was left behind. The driver cut right out in front of oncoming traffic as the car's rear-end fishtailed.

George turned and looked toward the diner's window at the table where he'd sat. The old woman watched him and smiled when their eyes met.

He didn't go back inside. He tucked his book in the back of his pants and hopped on his bike. He waited for traffic to clear then crossed the street.

9

GEORGE RODE BACK to Joyce's house and stopped behind a beat-up minivan he didn't recognize. It was dark out, and most of the lights were on inside the house.

He lifted the garage door, rolled his bike inside and leaned it against the shelves of boxes and storage bins. He looked up at the top shelf, glanced toward the door to the house and made sure Joyce wasn't about to stick her nose out.

He stretched toward the top shelf and pulled down the cardboard box with crumbled newspapers on top. He reached inside, pulled out some cash and stuck it in his pocket. He lifted Victor Albanese's championship belt from the box and stared at the emeralds and gold and what looked like diamonds on the outer edge. He had no idea what was fake and what was real.

The door creaked. He stuffed the belt back into

the box and threw it up on the top shelf. He pulled the garage door closed and went into the house through the front door.

Inside he pulled open the refrigerator and grabbed a can of beer. He stopped when he heard someone talking to Joyce out on the three-season porch.

He walked out and saw Joyce seated in a chair facing a man on the couch. George could only see the back of the man's head, but the man turned and looked over the back of the couch at George.

"*Jesus Christ!*" George said as he spit his beer over the top of the can.

The man stood, his hands down by his side. He stared back at George and with a nod said, "Miss me?"

George couldn't get a word out, looked over at Joyce and saw the look on her face he didn't like. She wasn't happy.

Not that she ever was.

"Earl? What the hell are you doing here? How'd you get out?"

Earl nodded, pointed towards Joyce with his thumb. "Joyce here was just tellin' me what a fine, law-abiding citizen you've been... workin' hard in the back of a pizza joint?"

George nodded.

Earl said, "Maybe you could get ole' Earl here a job. I make a fine pizza, you know." He winked at George and showed him a big smile.

George stepped further into the room.

Earl put out his arms. "Give the brother some love, will you?"

They hugged, slapped each other on the back as George looked toward Joyce.

Joyce gave him a look he didn't like.

"I must be losing my senses," Earl said as he turned to Joyce. He moved his head like his neck was stiff. "They used to say I was like a cat; could hear for miles away." He turned toward George. "You come in, I swear I didn't hear a peep. I mean, heard the garage all right... heard you crack that can of beer. Didn't hear no car, though."

"I don't have a car," George said.

Earl's eyebrows went high on his head. "You walk?"

"I got a bike."

"I didn't hear a bike, either. Guess it ain't no Harley?"

George stared back at Earl for a moment before he opened his mouth. "It's not a motorcycle. It's a bike... a bicycle."

Earl raised his eyebrows again and looked back at Joyce. "Your brother, he a grown man and still rides a bicycle, huh?"

Joyce stared back at Earl but didn't answer.

He stuck out his lower lip as he looked back and forth from George to Joyce and nodded. "Okay, okay. I see."

George said, "So if you don't mind me asking, Earl. What are you doing here?"

The smile dropped from Earl's face as he turned to George and tipped his head to the side. "Now what kinda question is that for an old friend?"

"Don't get me wrong. It's good to see you on the outside. I don't mean anything by it, I just... ."

Earl grabbed his throat with his long, boney fingers. "Man, my throat sure is dry." He gave George a look.

George's eyes moved toward the can of Coors Light under the lamp on the table, right next to where Earl was standing.

Joyce said as she got up from her chair. "Oh, I'm sorry. You want a beer?"

Earl waved his hand back and forth at Joyce. "Please, no. Sit down. I was merely suggesting George and I go out, grab ourselves a couple of cocktails." He glanced at the old digital clock underneath the TV. "The night is young, and we got some catching-up to do."

Joyce didn't sit back down but walked past Earl and right past George as she gave him a look. "I gotta get ready for work." She stepped toward the doorway.

Earl said, "So Joyce, what is it you do for work, if you don't mind me asking?"

She stopped and turned in front of the doorway. "I work at a nursing home."

Earl scratched the back of his neck as he nodded. "That's an admirable profession, I would say."

Joyce raised both her eyebrows. "It's actually not. It's quite depressing, if I can be honest. Nothing like taking care of old people with a foot in the grave... only time they'll leave is in a bag."

Joyce turned and disappeared through the doorway.

Earl looked back at George, his hands together behind his back. "She's just a ball of sunshine, ain't she?"

George sipped his beer, looked back at Earl over the top of the can. He hesitated a moment before he spoke. "You going to tell me the real reason you're here?"

Earl shrugged. "I need a reason? Don't know many people on the outside. You know that. Tell me —unless I was mistaken—I got the impression you and I were friends."

George kept his stare on Earl for a moment before he broke into a nod. "We were. I mean... we *are* friends. Of course. It's just..." George looked down at the top of his can of beer. "I'm trying to put my past life behind me."

Earl nodded. "I see." He looked around the room. "That why you're still sleeping on your big sister's couch?" He held his hands out—palms up—like a preacher at the head of the church. "This all what you call a *fresh start*?" He stepped toward George and put his arm over his shoulder. "I've missed talking to you, my friend. Not everyone I know thinks like you." He nodded his head toward the door. "Now, why don't you and me go grab us a couple cocktails... talk about putting this past of yours behind you."

George slipped out from under Earl's arm. "I've only been out a few weeks. A month, really." He smiled. "Didn't think you'd miss me so soon."

Earl scratched his temple with his long finger. "That all it's been?"

George finished the can of beer and placed the empty can back on the coffee table. "There's a bar down the street."

Earl smiled and turned for the door.

"Unless you want to ride on the back of my bike, you'll have to drive."

The inside of the minivan Earl was driving smelled like fried food or vomit. Maybe both. George rolled down the window.

"So you got out, what, a few days ago?"

Earl looked at him from the driver's seat and nodded.

"How'd you get the van?" George said as he pointed. "Turn here."

Earl kept his eyes on the dark road, turned the wheel and said, "Got it from the parking lot of the hardware store."

"It's stolen?"

Earl shrugged. "You expect me to go out, buy myself a vehicle? Pockets are beyond empty."

George said, "You driving without a license?"

Earl glanced at George. "What, you mister straight-as-an-arrow now? Like you some reformed goodie-two-shoes?"

George looked to his right and nodded toward the bar, a small, brick standalone building tucked back a ways from the road. "There it is."

Earl squinted his eyes, leaned over the steering wheel and looked up at the sign. "Chopmist Hill Inn, uh? You sure it's open?"

After a couple shots of Wild Turkey—Earl's choice —George started to loosen up a bit. They sat at a small table toward the back and drank beers. George had Budweiser, Earl a Miller on draft.

They talked about all the time they spent together in prison.

"I knew when you first walked in the place you were all right," Earl said. "Not normal to see a good-looking kid like yourself walk in, make it very far without, well... you know."

"I appreciated you always looking out for me. You know that, right Earl?"

Earl raised his pint of yellow beer and downed the whole damn thing without even taking a breath. His dark Adam's apple bounced up and down as he dumped the beer down his throat. He slapped the empty glass down on the table and gave an exaggerated, "Ahhhh" as he waved over toward the bartender. He held up the glass and tapped the side with that long finger, as if it had a mind of its own. He gave a nod to George. "I *did* say I was thirsty, didn't I?" He pushed his glass aside and leaned forward with his elbows down on the table. "You really think you can survive on the outside, you try to walk a straight line?" He gave George a look.

George didn't answer right away. He sipped his beer. "I have no interest in going back." He gave Earl a nod, "Can't imagine you do, either."

Earl leaned back in his chair. "Don't forget. I was in a lot longer than you. Half my life's been spent behind bars. Not that I'd trade it for my freedom, be able to sit down with a friend... have a few beers." Earl straightened himself out when the bartender came over to their table with two more beers. Earl took a sip, licked his lips. "But I know as well as anyone, man comes out of that system, the rest of your life's an uphill climb." He shrugged. "I don't care, you did three or twenty... you got a monkey on your back you'll never shake off."

The two sat quiet for a few moments, Earl turned in his chair and looked toward a couple of older women up at the bar. He turned back to George with the glass up in front of his lips. "You still dreaming about that pizza joint you said you'd open?"

George took a moment before he answered, "If I can somehow come up with enough money..."

Earl put his glass down on the table, leaned back with his hands together on his stomach. His long, skinny legs were stretched out straight under the table. He looked back at George, quiet.

"I just feel I still have time to turn my life around. I'm still relatively young."

Earl chewed the inside of his cheek as he watched George. Again he leaned forward on the table. "What if I told you I had a lead on something? Foolproof."

George let out a slight chuckle. "You know, I've been out a little over three weeks and you're the third person with a so-called lead, hoping to get me to cross that line."

"Cross that *line*?" Earl grabbed his beer and again straightened himself out in the chair. "You need money, right? You said it yourself. Unless you got something else up your sleeve, you ain't ever gonna make enough working in the back of a pizza joint, I can guarantee you that much." Earl cracked a slight smile as he tipped back the pint and finished off the rest of his beer.

He stood from his chair and went up to the bar, came back with two shot glasses filled with Wild Turkey. He slid one across the table to George and raised his glass. "To crossing that line." Earl winked at George, tipped his head back and emptied his glass.

George raised his, finished the Wild Turkey in one shot. He chased it with what was left of his beer and pushed the glasses aside. He was feeling good.

He leaned forward on the table, stared at Earl. And before he thought much about what he was doing, he went ahead and told Earl about the Championship belt he stole from Victor's house... and where they could get another one, might be worth a bit more.

10

AFTER A SHORT stop at Joyce's house so George could grab a few things, Earl pulled the minivan up along the road in front of Victor Albanese's driveway. He ducked his head down in front of George so he could see out the passenger-side window. "You sure there ain't nobody home?" he said as he straightened up behind the wheel.

George shrugged, the Wild Turkey—not to mention all the beers they drank—still in his head. "He's gone for a few more days, as far as I know."

Earl's face got twisted. "As far as you know?" He turned the minivan toward the driveway. "And the alarm don't work?"

George nodded. "I hear it's a bit outdated."

Earl said, "So, what... we leave the van right here?"

George turned too Earl. "Been a long time, huh? Like you're a virgin all over again."

"Twenty years, but I never messed around,

breaking into homes. When I was a kid, maybe. My thing was always, you go where you already know the money's at." He gave George a quick look. "Banks, armored cars..." Earl turned the headlights off as they drove toward the house, his chin just over the steering wheel with his eyes out toward the dark night in front of them. "You take the lead on this one, just tell me what to do."

George thought for a moment. "What about if I go in alone? You wait in the van."

Earl shook his head. "I ain't no *getaway* driver, like some goddamn sitting duck."

They pulled closer to the house, the muffler a little loud but otherwise the only sound was the pings off the undercarriage and the popping sound from the tires over the gravel.

"So you already been in there, huh? How do you know the cops ain't shown up?"

"I would've heard," George said. "We go in the same door I went in, get in and get out in ten minutes... tops."

Earl said, "You know where it is?"

"The belt?"

"Yeah, the belt. Unless there's more than one?"

George opened the passenger door and stepped out. "Keep it running, I'll go in, let the garage door up." He turned and walked along the brick walkway toward the house and up the steps. He pushed open the exterior door—no problem at all—and went inside.

He closed the door behind him, stood real still for a moment and listened. He was calm.

Inside the house, George walked straight through the kitchen and out into the garage. He slapped the button on the wall and watched as the opener cranked and the door went up.

Earl pulled the van inside and stuck his head out the driver side window. "This'd better be worth it," he said. "I'll tell you, there's something to be said for the ease of, you know, you just walk in and hand the pretty bank teller a note... she hands you a bag of money."

"I don't know, Earl. Times have changed since the last time you robbed a bank." George pulled a flashlight from his pocket and walked back into the house.

Earl followed behind him. He said, "So where you gonna find a buyer for a championship belt?"

"My brother-in-law. *Ex* brother-in-law."

They walked through the kitchen and down the hall with the lights off, George in front with his flashlight shined ahead of them along the floor.

"You never said nothin' about a three-way split," Earl said.

"Louie's the one who told me about the belts." He turned toward Earl. "In fact, it could end up being four-way."

"Jesus, George. You gotta be a little more upfront

about these things." Earl shook his head, looked down toward the floor. "Ain't gonna be nothin' left."

George walked down the stairs toward the basement. He looked back at Earl. "It'll be more than either of us have right now." At the bottom of the stairs he turned, shined his flashlight around and saw another display on the wall with an even bigger belt inside.

Earl put his hand against the glass. "I remember this one, you know. Knocked him out in the fifth round. Don't remember who it was—the other boxer..." He turned to George. "It was Manny Pampiano. That's right... guy's eyes spun in his head... like a slot machine before he went down."

George pulled his bag off his shoulder and dropped it on the ground. He pulled a long pry bar from the bag and with his hand backed Earl away from the glass. He cocked his arms back like he was in the batter's box and swung it hard into the glass. But it bounced off like a rubber ball. "Shit," he said as he whipped his hands up and down trying to relieve the sting.

Earl reached out his hand, took it out of George's hands. "Let me see that thing." He took a swing and the pry bar bounced off the glass.

"Can't break it." George took the pry bar back from Earl and jammed it between the display and the wall. "Got the one upstairs, no problem," he said. "Smashed the glass with one swing."

Earl rubbed his chin. "This one's more valuable, don't you think?"

George had the pry bar stuck behind the display, left it there as he reached into his bag. He pulled out a hammer and took a good swing, whacked the back of the pry bar. But the display didn't budge from the wall.

Earl walked toward the stairs, put his foot up on the bottom step and turned to George. "The other one was easy, huh?"

George nodded as he took another swing with his hammer. The hammer slipped off the pry bar, hit the corner of the case and knocked off a chunk of wood. George touched the edge where the wood broke and shined his flashlight on it. "It's steel," he said.

"Gotta be a way to get to it," Earl said.

"It's bolted to the wall. Probably has steel studs in the wall."

Earl stood with his hands on his hips, looking at the display. "Like a safe." Earl said.

George looked at his watch. "We've been here too long already."

"Maybe there's something in the garage we can use," Earl said.

George took another swing with the hammer and struck the pry bar, still stuck behind the case. He threw the hammer down at the floor. *"Goddamnit!"* He'd started coming down from his buzz. "Might be time to say goodnight, Earl."

"You serious? We just gonna leave? Walk away?" Earl started up the stairs. "I'm at least gonna go see what the old lady's got in her room."

"*Earl!*" George yelled as Earl disappeared into the darkness up the stairs. "*We don't have time, we gotta get out of here!*" George heard Earl's feet on the stairs above his head, heading up toward the bedrooms. "Shit." George looked back at the belt behind the glass, shook his head and with both hands tried again, this time freeing the pry bar from behind the case.

He threw his bag over his shoulder and ran up the stairs after Earl. He turned and stopped at the bottom of the stairs that went to the bedrooms upstairs. He didn't want to yell, but raised his voice enough so Earl could hear him. "Earl, where the hell are you? Let's get out of here. Forget about it." He closed his eyes for a moment but when he opened them, he saw a light shine from the master bedroom at the end of the hall upstairs.

George thought to himself, *this is why I work alone.*

And just as he said it, he saw a light bounce off the wall from outside. He turned and looked toward the window and right away knew what the light had come from. He yelled, "*Earl! It's the cops!*" He ducked and stayed low as he hurried to the back of the house. He made his way for the back door, stood up straight and yelled one more time, "*Earl, the cops are outside. We gotta go!"*

He waited as long as he could, then ran out the door. He turned away from the driveway and straight into the woods.

Once he was far enough away, he stopped and looked back toward the house. Blue lights flashed from the police car. He looked toward the far end of the driveway, toward the street, and saw another set of blue lights flashing as a car drove toward the house, up the long driveway.

George ran another fifty yards, stopped and turned again. He could barely see the house through the trees, but heard a cop yell, *"Freeze right there. Don't move!"* George turned and ran as fast as he could in the other direction. He ran as deep into the woods as he could, as fast as he could, as sticks and branches whipped him in the face... his own heavy breathing loud inside his head.

11

GEORGE SAT ON the couch as his foot bounced up and down on the floor at a rapid pace. His heart raced. His head pounded. And his feet hurt from all the running and he had scratches on his face from being in the woods.

He had already climbed up into the attic above the garage and hid the belt he took from Victor's the *first* time he broke in. He pulled up a piece of plywood and stuffed the belt between the floor joists under the pink insulation.

He must've checked his duffle bag at least ten times, made sure he hadn't left anything behind. He had the pry bar, his hammer, the flashlight... He couldn't think of anything else he could've left at Victor's. But he thought Earl might've grabbed something from George's bag, left it at the scene or had it in his hands when the cops showed up.

He didn't want to leave Earl behind like he did.

But he knew he had no choice. Maybe if he'd been sober, it would've been different. Although they probably wouldn't have been in there otherwise. *Why didn't Earl just stay in the damn van, out on the road? Who else saw them together at the bar?*

He knew Earl wouldn't talk. At least he didn't think so. But the more he thought about it... the more he thought Earl'd tell the cops about George...

He looked at the red numbers on the digital clock under the TV. *Four-thirty-seven.*

He was wide awake.

A door slammed out in front of the house. He jumped from the couch, headed for the back door.

It was Joyce, the last person he wanted to see.

He laid down on the couch, pulled the blanket up over his shoulder and turned on his side, his eyes wide open as he faced the back side of the couch.

George went out on his bike a little after the sun came up. He rode downtown, but not too sure where he was going.

As long as he wasn't in the house when Joyce rolled out of bed with her hair on fire and a stick up her ass.

He had his phone in his pocket, but he turned it off so he could avoid having to talk to anyone, at least until his hangover was gone. The truth was, a good part of the night was a little foggy. But one thing he knew was things weren't good.

He was on his bike in the middle of the road when a horn blew behind him. He didn't look back as he took his bike up onto the sidewalk with his hand up to wave for the car to pass.

But the horn blew again. George looked and saw Louie, pulled over in his old, black Lincoln with the beige vinyl roof. He put the window down and gave George a nod as he parked on the wrong side of the road in front of George.

Louie stepped out onto the sidewalk. "Where've you been? You hear about Victor Albanese's house?"

George stared back at him, quiet. He shook his head.

"Caught a guy... broke into Victor's house. Walked out with a pillowcase full of the girlfriend's jewelry."

"Girlfriend?" George said, as if that piece of information mattered.

Louie nodded. "Yeah, that's what they said."

"He's not married?"

Louie gave him a funny look then shrugged. "Who cares?"

George thought about the first bedroom he opened, the room with the pink walls... thought it would've been Victor's daughter's room although he was a little old to have a daughter with pink walls.

Not that it mattered.

Louie said, "Really puts the shits on our plan to get those belts... no chance we'd ever get in there now."

George nodded, kind of a blank stare on his face. "Are you out looking for me, or you just happen to —"

"I saw the house'd been broken into, before they mentioned they caught someone. I thought maybe it was..." He paused and looked off, then turned back to George. "Honestly, I thought for a second maybe it was you or—"

"Me?" He shook his head. "Nope."

Louie looked back and forth along the road as a couple of cars drove by. He again turned to George. "So where were you last night?"

George's heart raced. His blood pumped in his neck. He shrugged. "I don't know. Around."

Louie reached back into his car, grabbed a cigarette pack off the dashboard and stuck one in his mouth. "Joyce tell you I stopped by?" He lit the cigarette and took a drag as he looked back at George through the smoke.

"No, I haven't seen her."

Louie took a drag and kept his eyes on George, then turned and opened the car door. "I've got a meeting later this morning. I'll tell you more about it later." He stepped into the car, pulled the door closed and hung his arm out the window. "Where you goin' now, anyway?" He nodded toward the bike. "You and that friggin' bike..." He pulled away without saying another word.

George took his bike all the way to Roger Wheeler Park and sat on a bench along the lake. He watched the runners and walkers and mothers with strollers pass by on the track around the water.

He was surprised when a woman ran past him he knew he recognized. *No way*, he thought as he got up from the bench and jumped on his bike.

He rode after her, but stayed back and watched as she ran at a good pace ahead of him.

He finally took his bike up next to her, rode alongside her and turned to make sure it was really her. He slowed to let the bike coast. "Sam?"

She took a quick glance at him, but kept running ahead.

He pulled up ahead of her and looked back, over his shoulder. "Sam? It's me, George."

She stopped and and smiled through her heavy breathing as he rode ahead then circled back to where she stood. She pulled the earbuds from her ears. "Hey," she said. "What are you doing here?" She looked down at his bike.

"I swear, I'm not stalking you," he said. But as soon as he did, he wished he hadn't.

She gave him a look, her eyebrows raised on her head.

He nodded toward the bench. "I saw you run by."

"Sorry, I didn't even see you." She held up the

earbuds. "Kind of in my own world when I come out here."

"No, that's okay. I wasn't sure it was you."

"Hey, I wanted to say I was sorry for the other night. I didn't mean to cut you short."

George knew what she meant, but wanted to play it cool. "The other night?"

She nodded. "That was my ex-boyfriend. I needed a ride, and he was the only one who could—"

"He's your *ex*-boyfriend?"

She looked down toward the ground for a moment, looked up at George and nodded as she pushed a strand of hair from her face.

There was an awkward silence between them as they stood in the middle of the track with everyone else having to walk around them.

"We should probably get out of the way," Sam said as she started to walk away, toward the grass.

He got off his bike and walked with it next to her. They were quiet again until he spoke up. "You think we can grab a coffee? I don't mean now... unless you want to. Maybe one morning, or—"

She nodded. "Yes, of course. I don't know about right now, though." She pulled at her shirt with her fingers. "I'm a little sweaty." She turned and looked George in the eye as they walked side-by-side.

"You look fine," he said. "If you want to go now, I'm not doing anything. I was going to go over to Bravos Cafe, over at Founders Square."

"The place with the cobblestone patio?"

He nodded. "Yeah, that's it."

Sam said, "You mind if I finish my run and I'll meet you there?" She looked at her watch, squeezed the buttons on the side and looked back at George. "Half hour?"

"You want me to wait for you?"

She shrugged. "You like to run?"

George shook his head, looked down at his bike. "Not unless the cops are after me."

Samantha gave him a look and didn't smile. "I'll meet you there in a half hour, okay?"

He stepped back on his bike and gave her a thumbs-up, turned his bike around in the opposite direction and almost into a group of oncoming runners. He rode his bike off the track and headed for Bravos.

12

GEORGE WAITED FOR Sam to show up at the cafe, pulled his phone from his pocket and turned it on for the first time all day. It made him anxious. He preferred being out of touch, and missed the old days when landlines and payphones were the only option.

The message indicator came on right away. He pressed the button to listen to the first message. It was Joyce asking where he was—as if he could answer her through voicemail—and that she wanted him to call her right away. The message was a few hours old.

He deleted it from his phone.

There was another message. This time from Roy:

Hey man, call me as soon as you get this. Don't know where you are or what you've heard about... just call me back, I'll tell you about it."

George deleted Roy's message and was relieved

there weren't any others. Especially from Earl... his one phone call from jail.

He put his phone away and sipped his coffee as he turned in his seat to make sure his bike was still where he'd left it, against the brick wall on the side of Bravos cafe.

It'd been more than a half hour, maybe forty minutes, since he saw Sam. But she hadn't shown up yet.

He had a good feeling about her. He liked her, he thought. At least from what he knew of her so far. She was good looking and seemed happy, from what he could tell. He thought about the ex-boyfriend.

What an odd match.

His mind had wandered when she walked up to his table and grabbed a chair that scraped across the cobblestone when she pulled it from under the table. "Sorry," she said as she sat down across from him. "I lost track of time." She pulled at her sweaty t-shirt from the front. "I warned you, didn't I?" Her face was beat-red, her hair moist on the ends.

George stood from his seat. "What can I get you?"

She shook her head and pushed her chair back. "No, please... I'll get it." She got up and started toward the door and turned to him. "Do you want anything else?"

George held up his cup and shook his head as he eased back into his seat. He watched Samantha walk inside the cafe until a police vehicle out on the street caught his eye. He pulled his sunglasses down over his eyes and slouched down in his chair.

Samantha came back out with her paper cup with the strings from tea bags hanging down the side. She must've cleaned up—her hair up on her head and her face not so sweaty and red like it was when she showed up.

She sat down and said, "So tell me... what do you do for work?"

He started to nod, turned it into a shake and did what he could to avoid giving her much of an answer. "I work for a friend." He tried to turn it around. "What about you?" he said. But as soon as the words left his mouth he realized how dumb he sounded. "I'm sorry. I know. You work at the diner."

"Actually, I'm a student. I'm in school, working on my master's in social work."

"Social work, huh?" He nodded as if he approved. "That's great. Most people today are so goddamn focused on making money..." He stopped himself. "I'm sorry, I didn't mean... not that you can't make money in social work... I'm just saying, money's not everything, right?" He looked down toward the table. "I'll shut up."

"No, you're right... I didn't choose a path that had anything to do with money." She shrugged and she put her cup of tea up to her mouth. "It's just not that important to me."

George smiled. "You get that a lot? Tell someone

you're in social work and they look at you like you've taken a vow of poverty?"

Samantha smiled. "Maybe one day I'll go into private practice... if I ever get sick of Ramen noodles."

George looked over his cup as he sipped his coffee. "You ever actually eat them?"

She laughed. "I've actually never tried them. Don't think I will. But isn't that what everyone says?"

George stuck the wooden stirrer in his mouth, between his teeth.

"So what about you?" she said. "What do you do for your friend?"

He didn't want to answer. "I don't know, it's just..."

"You don't know what you do?" She gave him a look.

"No, it's not that. He owns a restaurant. He's just someone I've known for a long time... I help him out." He tried to make it sound like he was doing Frank a favor working for him. "I'd like to open a place one day. Trying to save up some money."

"You mean... your own business?"

George nodded. "A restaurant."

She stared back at him, as if waiting for him to continue.

He looked toward the back of the cafe. "Maybe something like this. Small and simple, you know?"

"I grew up in the restaurant business," she said.

"The diner?"

Samantha pushed the chair back from the table and crossed her legs.

George tried not to look at them but couldn't help himself. She wasn't exactly thin—not like a rail, anyway—and had nice legs. Somewhat thick with muscle.

"That was my aunt at the diner the other night. She said she almost waited on you before you left... when I saw you outside."

"She's your aunt?"

Sam smiled. "She thought you were cute."

George tried to hold in a smile, but couldn't help himself. "I should've left her my number."

"I don't know if that would've gone over well with my uncle." She sipped her tea, holding the cup with both hands. "She asked who you were... how I knew you. I told her I didn't know you."

They sat quiet for a moment as George turned and looked toward the street. Another police vehicle cruised by on the street.

"They here for you?" Samantha said as she followed George's eyes toward the vehicle, her eyebrows high on her head.

"Huh?" George shook his head and shrugged, pretending he didn't hear her.

"I'm just kidding." She cracked half a smile—her eyes on George with his sunglasses down over his eyes. "You're not a murderer, are you?"

George turned toward her as he straightened his

sunglasses on his face. "Me?" He shook his head. "Not normally."

"My father's a retired cop."

George felt as if someone had poured cold water down his pants. "A cop, huh? Around here?"

She shook her head and leaned forward, her elbows on the table as she picked at the cardboard sleeve around her cup. "He's down in Florida. My parents live in Tampa Bay."

"How come you're up here?" George said. "For school?"

"My aunt was sick, so I moved up here to help her while I attended school."

"She's okay now?"

Samantha nodded. "It was bad for a while. But she's healthy now. I used to come up here in the summers—my whole family would—and as I got older I'd work at the diner over the summer months." She smiled. "My aunt and I have always been close."

George sat quiet, stared across the table at her and admired her good looks.

"You ever want to talk to my uncle about the restaurant business, just let me know. He loves to talk about it... that diner's his baby."

"Maybe," George said. His mind had gone somewhere else. He thought about her father, the retired cop. He looked at his watch. "I hate to leave, but I'm going to have to—"

"Do you have a car, or do you ride a bike everywhere you go?" She looked past him at his bike against the side of the building.

"I had a car but..." He didn't finish. "I like to ride. Keeps me in shape."

"What do you do when it's cold, in the winter?" she said.

George shrugged. "Florida sounds nice."

They both got up from the table.

"Maybe we can do this again?" he said.

She smiled and nodded. "You know where to find me." She turned and walked toward the street, turned the corner and disappeared.

13

ROY WAS IN the parking lot at Frank's Place when George rode in on his bike. He was there before he had to be to work, the only other vehicle in the lot besides Roy's was Frank's Corvette.

Roy stepped out of his van. "I've been calling you all night. Even this morning. Where've you been?"

George pushed his bike in through the back door of the restaurant. "I had my phone off, just got your message on the way here." He leaned his bike against the wall just inside the door and turned to Roy just behind him. "Is something wrong?"

"Didn't you listen to my message?"

"Most of it."

"You hear me say something was wrong?"

"I guess so." George knew exactly what was up, but still said, "So why don't you tell me?"

George walked past the boxes and restaurant supplies in the back room of the restaurant and into the kitchen. He heard Frank out in the front of the restaurant.

Roy followed. "I went by Joyce's looking for you. She was pissed, said she had no idea where you were and you weren't answering your phone."

George smiled. "See? It wasn't just you."

Roy looked around, poked his head out toward the dining area where Frank was getting the place ready to open. He turned back to George and in a hushed tone said, "Victor Albanese's house got hit last night. Someone broke in. I guess they caught him."

George said, "Where'd you hear all this?" He didn't let on that Louie'd already told him the same thing. Roy folded his arms at his chest, leaned against the stainless steel table with the deli slicer George used to cut meat behind him. "They took him into custody, guess they caught him red-handed, holding Victor's wife's jewelry... filled a pillow case."

"You sure it was his wife's?" George said, knowing Victor wasn't married.

Roy shrugged. "I don't know. What's the difference?"

George didn't answer as he stepped toward the walk-in cooler and went inside, came out with a cardboard case of lettuce. He lifted the case up onto the stainless steel table.

Roy said, "If I can be honest, George... when I first heard his house was broken into, I thought for a second you mighta gone in there without me."

Frank walked in from the front part of the restaurant. He gave Roy a nod, turned to George. "Don't your friends do anything besides hang around my kitchen?" He gave Roy a look out of the corner of his eye.

"Hey, what'd *I* do?" Roy said, staring back at Frank.

Frank handed him a broom. "You gonna hang around, why don't you make yourself useful?"

Roy put his hands up in the air, backpedaled a few steps. "I got my own work to take care of."

Frank looked back and forth from Roy to George. "You two hear about Victor Albanese's house? Got broken into."

Roy nodded. "I was just telling George. Caught the guy already, too. Red-handed, holding onto one of Victor's belts."

George had his back to Roy and Frank, as if he wasn't listening. But he'd heard every word, knew Roy had it wrong. He turned to Frank and Roy. "Did you say they caught him with a belt? A championship belt?"

Roy nodded. "I think so."

George stared him in the eye. "You sure?"

Roy shrugged. "Just going by what I heard."

"Wonder what that thing's worth?" Frank said. He leaned the broom behind the refrigerator, stepped to the stainless steel sink and washed his hands. Over his shoulder, he said, "Wouldn't be surprised something like that goes for a few hundred grand. Heard that's what some of 'em are worth." He wiped his hands on a towel he had draped over his shoulder. "I'm sure Victor'll be happy, they got it back."

George said, "Doesn't sound like Roy knows whether or not they caught the guy with the belt or not."

There was a knock at the entrance, like someone used something hard to whack the glass door.

Frank shook his head. "Don't these friggin' people know how to read the sign?" He looked at his watch. "Don't open for twenty minutes." He walked out of the kitchen and headed out front. He turned back, stuck his head through the doorway. "George, it's your sister."

George wiped his hands on his smock and walked out to the front of the restaurant. The lights were still off, although the light from the sun kept the place well lit.

Joyce knocked again. She turned with her back to the door and faced the parking lot, not even looking toward George through the glass door.

He turned the lock and pushed the door open.

"Where the hell were you last night?" she said as soon as she walked in the door, a real bite to her voice.

George looked back toward the kitchen, grabbed Joyce by the arm, pushed open the door and pulled her outside. "Keep your voice down," he said. "This is Frank's place of business."

She ripped her arm from his grasp. "Keep your hands off me." She folded her arms at her chest. "Are you going to tell me? Did you do it?"

George's face got a bit twisted. "Did I do *what*?"

"Break into that house? With that *con*-vict who showed up at my house last night?"

George stared back at her, not saying a word as he leaned against the brick exterior next to the door. "No. I wasn't with him. We got a drink, then he left."

"Where'd you go?"

"I was on the couch, sleeping."

"Before that. I came home on my break, you weren't home."

George was quick. "You must not've seen me. What time?"

She shrugged. "I don't know. A little after two."

"I met someone at the bar. Earl left, said he didn't want to be the third wheel. I had no idea where he went."

"Well, I'll tell you where he went. He went to Victor Albanese's house, that's where he went."

She stared back at George, her eyes narrowed. "Don't lie to me, George."

"Why would I lie to you? You think I give a shit what you think?"

She cocked her head, the fat under her chin bunched up and blended in with the rest of her neck. "You don't care what I think?"

George looked at her, thought how she looked like their father when he'd get pissed... or whenever he was drunk, which was whenever he was awake.

She turned to walk away, stopped at the edge of the parking lot and looked back at George, her long finger pointed right towards his face. "Get your shit out of my house. In fact, I'm changing the goddamn locks. How's that sound? Keep you *and* Louie out of my house for good."

"Louie? What'd *he* do?"

"I'm sick of him walking in like he still lives there." She turned and stormed off, got in her car and slammed the door. She started the engine and squealed the tires as she backed out of her parking spot. The car spun as it caught some of the dirt on the asphalt. The rear end of her car fishtailed as she hit the street.

George shook his head as he watched her car disappear. He turned and walked back inside, locked the door behind him, and walked back into the kitchen.

Frank stepped into the kitchen. "Is Joyce *ever* in a good mood?" he said.

George just shook his head, got right to work cutting the lettuce on the steel table.

Roy walked around the corner as if he came out of nowhere, but was listening. "We were always scared of her, even when we were kids."

Frank walked back out to the front then stuck his

head through the doorway. "George, I need you to make a sauce."

Roy looked toward the dining area out front where Frank was, stepped toward George. "I was outside and couldn't help overhear you and Joyce."

George lifted the heavy, one-hundred-forty-quart stock pot up onto the gas stove. He grabbed the wooden matches and lit the gas burner underneath the pot as blue flames shot up around the bottom. He had his back to Roy as he adjusted the flame with the knob... not saying a word.

"What was that Joyce said about a friend you went out with last night? Something about a convict?"

George grabbed the square can of olive oil and dumped it into the pot, pulled a glass jar of chopped garlic from the fridge and dumped it inside with the oil. He heard what Roy had said, but worked as if he wasn't there.

Roy said, "You hear me?"

George turned, looked at Roy over his shoulder. "Yeah, what... I don't know what Joyce was talking about, she—"

"Who was she talking about? Someone you went out for drinks with?"

George brushed past Roy, grabbed a large can of crushed tomatoes, ran it under the industrial-sized can opener just above the stainless steel table and opened the can, dumped it in the pot. He grabbed another can, opened the top and dumped that one in. "Roy, what are you... my jealous girlfriend? Do I have to check in with you when I go out for drinks?"

Roy shook his head. "Unh uh, George. Don't bullshit me, man. Tell me the truth. Who was it?"

George opened another few cans of crushed tomatoes, walked back and forth from the table to the stove as he stepped past Roy, standing in the middle of the narrow kitchen in George's way.

Roy said, "Do you know that guy who broke into Victor's house?"

George grabbed another can of crushed tomatoes, slammed the can hard on top of the stainless table and turned to Roy. "I don't even know what you're talking about... I don't know a thing about who broke into that house, other than what you told me. Christ, Roy, why don't you leave me alone?"

Roy threw up his hands. "Okay, okay. Sorry... I was just asking."

Frank came around the corner. "What's going on back here? What's with all the yelling?" He looked at George. "Why's everybody breaking your balls today?"

14

GEORGE WENT TO Joyce's house after work, prayed she hadn't yet changed the locks like she said she would. But George knew, when Joyce said she was going to do something—especially when it was out of spite—she usually did it.

She wasn't home. George slid his key in the lock but it would barely make it into the lock. He looked at his key and wondered if it was the right one. He tried it again, but it didn't work.

He wasn't about to call her at work, beg her to let him in so he could get his things. Joyce spent most of her life in a bad mood, and when she was at work at the nursing home, she was even worse.

George stepped away from the front door, walked toward the garage and reached down for the handle to see if he could pull it open. He couldn't imagine she had the garage door lock changed, too. He didn't think she normally locked it.

But this time, she had.

He walked around the side of the garage and looked through the window. It crossed his mind to smash the glass but of course he'd have to pay for it. Although it might be worth it, considering he didn't know if the belt he hid in the attic was worth something.

As much as he knew it was a mistake and regretted taking it in the first place, he had to get the belt out of there, get it sold as soon as he could. He'd need Louie for that, which meant telling Louie and Roy the truth at some point.

Just not yet.

George had nowhere to go. *Jesus, Joyce*, he thought. *Doesn't take much to set her off.* He leaned toward the spotlight on top of the garage and looked down at his watch. It was after ten. The air had cooled. He wished he'd already called Louie ahead of time, asked if he could crash at his apartment.

He grabbed his bike and rode out toward the street. He wasn't exactly sure where he was going, but knew he'd figure it out. He'd call Frank... if he really had to.

Headlights shined past him from behind. He turned and looked over his shoulder but he couldn't see much of anything. The lights were too bright. He shielded his eyes with his forearm and squinted as the car continued toward him, going no faster than he was on his bike.

He saw the canned lights on the roof as the car pulled up beside him. The driver's side window went down.

Dawn was behind the wheel. "If I didn't know better, I'd say you were up to something." They both stopped as she shifted the car into park and leaned her elbow out the window, over the door.

"Why do I get the feeling you'd love to bust me just for being back on the outside," George said.

Dawn stared back at him for a moment before she spoke. "Is that what you think? I'm out to *get* you?"

George hesitated a moment but then didn't respond. "You work nights now?" He tried to play it cool.

"I picked up the shift for a friend. His wife had a baby."

George nodded, looked up over the roof. "Slow night, huh?"

She shrugged. "There's some whispering going on at the station about you."

"Oh yeah?" George tried not to swallow, thought about it so much it almost made him choke. He waited to hear what else she had to say.

"Word is, you're friends with Earl Christie."

George shrugged. "Name rings a bell, but—"

"Don't bullshit me, George."

He looked off for a moment. "I wouldn't use the word '*friends.*' "

"Someone spoke with the guards at the ACI, said

you two were pretty tight."

"I got along with the right people. Nothing more to it," George said.

Dawn turned and looked inside her car when dispatch came over the radio. She looked back out toward George. "Well, your friend Earl's behind bars. He broke into Victor Albanese's home and stole a championship belt. When they caught him coming out of the home, he had a pillowcase full of jewelry. The belt was nowhere to be found."

George stared right at Dawn, didn't say a word.

"So there's a theory," she said, "he didn't do it alone."

George put one leg over his bike, more than ready to get away from Dawn and her questions. "Are you trying to ask me if I had something to do with it?"

Dawn straightened out in the driver's seat. "It wouldn't make me happy to have to look up in my rearview, see you in my back seat again." She slapped the shifter on the column, kept her eyes straight ahead and drove away.

It was after midnight when George got off his bike outside of Louie's apartment. He went up the back stairs to the third floor and knocked on the door.

Louie was normally awake into the early morning hours, but he didn't come to the door. At least not right away.

George knocked again and the door swung open.

Louie had on a pair of boxers, but no shirt. His hair stuck up in all directions as he scratched his head. "Hey, George. I'm sorry, man... but now's not a good time." He leaned his head out the doorway, looked past George at the driveway below. "What the hell are you doing here?"

A middle-aged woman George had recognized from Keenan's bar slipped her head under the arm Louie had extended straight out as he held open the door. She giggled, held a martini glass with two hands and took a sip as she looked out at George over the rim.

"I told you to wait in the bedroom," Louie said, shaking his head. "Christ." He pushed open the door and gestured with his hand for George to come in. "You remember Candice?"

George looked back at her but didn't answer.

"I've seen you at Keenan's," she said with a high-pitched, somewhat squeaky voice.

Louie held open the refrigerator door and pulled out two Rolling Rock bottles. He turned back toward George. "You want a drink?"

Candice had a long Yankees t-shirt on that barely hung down to her thick thighs.

Louie looked her up and down with disgust. "Go get some pants on, will you?" He gave George a look and again shook his head. He tapped his finger on the side of his head. "This broad... nothin' upstairs." He lit a cigarette and took a drag.

"I'm sorry to show up like this. I tried your phone, but you didn't answer."

"Yeah, no shit," Louie said. "What the hell's going on? I don't even know what time it is."

George took a sip of beer and leaned back against the counter. "Joyce threw me out... changed the locks."

"What the hell'd you do now? Not that it takes much to set her off."

"I didn't do a thing."

"Nothing? You had to've done *something*, no? Your own sister tosses you out on the street in the middle of the night?"

George looked down the hall toward Louie's bedroom. He saw the door was closed. "I can't talk about it right now. Not while she's here."

Louie stared back at George for a moment, put his cigarette down in the brown, glass ashtray on the counter and walked down the hall, toward his bedroom. He knocked on the door. "Hey, Candice, you dressed yet?"

She didn't answer.

"Candice, you awake in there? I hope you're not in my bed."

You could hear the water running through the pipes.

Louie opened the bedroom door and yelled in at

Candice, "Hey, I told you to put on some pants... you go in and take a shower?" He walked back out to the kitchen, grabbed his cigarette from the ashtray and took a drag. He sipped what was left of his beer and put the bottle down in the sink. He opened the fridge and grabbed another, held a Rolling Rock toward George, "You want another?"

George held his beer up—he'd hardly made a dent —shook his head. "I'm okay."

They were both quiet for a moment. Louie said, "So where you staying?"

George hesitated a moment before he answered. "I didn't realize you had a guest, but I was—"

"Candice?" He laughed as he pointed with his thumb toward the hall. "You think I'd want to wake up in the morning, have *that* sleeping next to me?" He pointed with his bottle toward the other room. "Not the most comfortable couch, but it's all yours if you want it."

15

GEORGE SAT UP from Louie's couch as Candice walked by, opened the door off the kitchen, and slammed it behind her. He picked up his watch off the floor and turned it toward the glow from the streetlight shining through the horizontal blinds.

He squinted his eyes. It was just after five in the morning.

He laid back on the couch with his hands together behind his head. The cigarette smell was strong in Louie's apartment. It reminded George of his house growing up, how his father always smelled like cigarettes and cheap cologne... breath permanently stained with the Pabst Blue Ribbon he downed by the twelve pack.

George's mother was just like Joyce. Bitter and always unhappy. Not that he could blame her... damaged by a husband not much different than Louie.

He wished he could fall back asleep, but the noise outside was too much. Cars moved along the early, morning streets. Broken mufflers and loud music filled the air, as did the sounds of bottles being dumped outside to hide the prior night's sins.

George sat up on the edge of the couch, still in the same clothes he'd had on the night before. He thought maybe he should go, but wanted to use Louie's shower—the one attached to Louie's bedroom.

He got up off the couch, went into the kitchen and opened each cabinet door. He needed a coffee, and found the Chock Full O' Nuts in the big yellow can.

Louie walked in the kitchen, his hair wet and slicked straight back. He gave George a nod, not saying much beyond a grumble as he grabbed a pack of cigarettes from the table and stuck a smoke in his mouth. He didn't light it right away. He poured himself a coffee, filled half his cup with heavy cream from the fridge then dumped at least three tablespoons of sugar over the top. He turned to George, seated at the table. He stared at him for a moment. "You look like shit."

George held up the cup of coffee he had in front of him. *"How do you drink this shit?"*

Louie sipped from his cup and shrugged. "I think it's good."

George forced the rest of his coffee down and got

up from the table. "You mind if I take a shower?"

"Make it fast. Gas prices are up."

George was quiet for most of the ride to Joyce's house. He'd look at Louie behind the wheel—more than once... close to telling him the truth about Earl and how he was right there with him at Victor Albanese's.

But realized it wouldn't do much other than let George get something off his chest.

George said, "I hope you can convince her to let me in the house."

Louie kept his eyes on the road as he turned onto Joyce's street. "You say that as if she listens to me. Or anyone, for that matter."

He pulled in the driveway and parked behind Joyce's car, turned off the engine and opened the door to step outside. "Wait here, I'll see if I can talk some sense into her." He got out and walked to her front door, walked right in, did exactly what Joyce told George she didn't like.

George watched from the car, thought about taking a nap, but needed to get in and get his clothes. He had no idea how he was going to get Victor's belt out of the attic space above the garage. He looked as Louie stuck his head out the front door, waved for George to come in.

"Everything all right?" George said as he walked

up the steps.

Louie held the door for him but didn't answer.

George walked past him and inside. He looked at Joyce as she leaned against the counter with a bag of frozen peas up against her face. George turned to the doorway and gave Louie a look. "What the hell happened?"

Louie shrugged. "Don't look at me. *I* didn't do it."

Joyce pulled the bag of frozen peas from her eye and looked at George. "I knew I should've never let you stay here."

George saw her swollen eye. "Jesus Christ, Joyce. Will you just tell me what the hell happened?"

"Your friend," she said. "That's what happened. The goddamn bank robber." She pressed the bag against her eye.

Louie cocked his head back, his eyebrows low over his eyes as he looked back and forth from George to Joyce. "What *bank robber*?"

"You mean, Earl?" George said. "Couldn't have been Earl. He's in jail."

Joyce pulled the bag of frozen peas away from her face. "Uh, that's where you're wrong. He's not in jail. Because he was standing right there." She nodded toward the floor where Louie stood in front of the door. She looked at George with her one good eye. "He was looking for you. I told him I had no idea where you were, that you weren't staying here anymore." She shrugged. "He didn't believe me."

Louie stood next to Joyce, tried to look close at her eye but she didn't move the bag. He turned to George. "What the hell's going on? Who's this guy?" He pointed with his thumb over his shoulder, toward Joyce, "Hits a woman?"

Joyce said, "Who the hell are you to talk?" Her eyes narrowed as she stared back at Louie.

"What's that mean? I never laid a hand on you. Not that it didn't cross my mind."

"Listen," George said. "Did you call the cops?"

She looked around. "You see any cops?"

George rolled his eyes. "It's just a question."

She shook her head. "He told me, if I call them I'd be making an error in judgement."

George closed his eyes for a brief moment, turned and looked out the window toward the front of Joyce's yard. "I'm sorry, Joyce, I—"

She put up her free hand. "Save it, you dumbass."

"What else did this clown say to you?" Louie said.

Joyce shrugged. "I told you, he wanted to know where George was." She glanced at George. "He said you set him up."

"Set him up?" Louie folded his arms at his chest and looked George right in the eye. "You gonna tell me what the hell's going on?"

George stepped across the kitchen and pulled out a chair at the small table in the corner. He sat down with his elbows rested on the table, put his head down in his hands.

Louie said, "So what are you going to do now, cowboy?"

George looked up, gave Louie a look. He took a moment, then said, "Can you get me a gun?"

"A gun?" Louie shrugged. "Of course I can." He turned and nodded toward Joyce. "What about you? You want a piece? For protection?"

She shook her head. "Why would you even ask me that? You know I don't like guns in my house. In fact, I don't want either of you in my house anymore. All you do is bring me grief. As long as you two assholes've been a part of my life, I've had to deal with nothing but shit, day after day." She shook her head, looked down at George seated at the table. "The only peace I had was when you were locked up in the can."

She walked toward the front door and pulled it open. With her hand on the knob she said, "Get out. Both of you."

"But Joyce..." George stood from the chair. "Who's going to protect you? I don't know if—"

"You think I need *you* to take care of me?" She laughed. "You're thirty-seven years old, sleeping on your sister's couch. That piece of shit friend of yours comes back here, I'll put a knife right through his throat."

Louie cracked a slight smile, but knew she wasn't joking. He was married to her long enough he knew she wasn't kidding around.

"He's not my friend," George said as Joyce pushed him through the door from behind.

Louie turned to Joyce. "You can at least let him get his things, no?"

She stared back at him for a moment before she answered. "Everything he left here is out in the garage."

Louie rolled his eyes and gave Joyce a nod with his chin. "By the way, I think you're overreacting."

She pointed to herself with her finger in her chest. "*I'm* overreacting? This man comes in my house, whacks me in the face... and you tell me *I'm* overreacting?"

"No, I mean... towards me and George, we—"

She pointed toward the door. "Ok, then you can get the hell out of my house. Or I *will* call the goddamn cops."

George stepped back into the house and past Joyce. He opened the other door across the kitchen and stepped down into the garage. He turned as Louie walked in behind him. "Joyce, was Earl alone?"

She shook her head. "There was someone else in the car with him. But he didn't come in. He or she... I wasn't sure."

"What kind of car?" Louie said.

"How the hell do I know? Do I look like some kind of mechanic? How do I know what kind of car it was? It was a piece of shit, the muffler making all kinds of noise. It had a white vinyl roof... that's all I really saw."

She slammed the door closed behind them and they stood in darkness for a moment until the light came on.

"*Thanks a lot, Joyce!*" Louie yelled toward the door, as if she could even hear him.

George looked around for the step stool he used to get into the attic, but he didn't see it anywhere. In fact, most of the boxes on the shelves were gone, including the original box he used to hide his belt and the money he took from Victor.

"What are you looking for?" Louie said. He nodded toward the duffle bag on the concrete floor. "Isn't that your bag?"

George didn't answer Louie, bent over and picked it up and threw it over his shoulder.

16

LOUIE HAD ONE arm out the window, the other on the steering wheel with a cigarette between his fingers. He turned and looked at George, held his stare on him for a moment. "So you gonna tell me the story with this guy?"

The wind blew in George's face on the passenger side as he stared straight ahead, toward the road. He looked at his reflection in the side view mirror as he answered Earl. "If he's out on bail, then it's just a matter of time."

"But you don't know?" Louie said.

"Don't know *what?*"

"That he's out on bail."

George turned to Louie. "I can't imagine he escaped, if that's what you mean?"

Louie flicked his cigarette out the window.

George turned from the passenger seat and looked toward the rear of the car. "You're going to light a fire, toss a lit cigarette out like that. It hasn't rained in three weeks."

Louie gave George a look. "What are you, *Smokey the Bear*?"

George scratched his head and looked out the window.

Louie said, "You still haven't told me the deal... the story with Earl."

George still didn't answer, felt the wind on his face as he leaned his head out the open window.

"Don't play games with me, George. Okay?" Louie grabbed another cigarette from his shirt pocket without removing the pack, stuck it in his mouth. "He whacks your sister like that, we oughta do something about it. But you gotta tell me... why he's looking for you, no?"

"We were in the can together."

"What'd you, do something to piss him off on the inside?"

George stared at himself in the side view mirror. He hesitated as he thought about what to tell Louie.

Finally, he turned and rolled up the window. "I was out with him the night he was arrested."

Louie kept his eyes on the road, quiet for a moment. "Were you with him at Victor Albanese's house?"

Right away, George shook his head. "No, we got some drinks. Then I went back to Joyce's." He shrugged. "I went to bed."

Louie paused a moment, kept his eyes on the road. "Then why'd he tell Joyce you set him up?"

"I don't know. He's not all there... upstairs."

"You tell him?"

"About Victor?" George thought for a moment. "I wish I hadn't, but..."

Louie shook his head, glanced toward George. "Shit, George. What'd you go and do that for?"

George didn't answer. He pulled open the glove box and reached inside, lifted the owner's manual and underneath was a brown paper bag with a 9mm inside. George pulled the gun out of the bag.

"Put that back, will you?" Louie said as he reached across and grabbed the gun, stuck it back in the glove box and slammed the door closed in front of George. "I'll get you one. I got a feeling you're gonna need it."

George called Frank and said he wouldn't be able to make it in, told him if anybody'd come looking for him, say he hadn't heard from him.

"You in trouble?" Frank said.

"I don't know. I might be." George hung up and stared out the passenger window toward the green awning over the door of Keenan's bar.

Louie parked right out front on the street, turned off the engine and stepped out. He slammed the door behind him and headed for the bar.

But George sat still in the passenger seat. He hadn't moved... stared straight ahead.

"You coming?" Louie said as he looked back at George with his hand on the door to Keenan's. He turned and walked inside before George answered.

George got out and walked inside behind Louie.

Jake was behind the bar. He had his chin up with his eyes on George as he approached him. Jake leaned forward on the bar with his thick arms spread wide from his broad shoulders. With a single nod, he cracked a crooked smile and said, "Where's your bicycle?"

George gave him a look and sat down on the stool next to Louie.

Louie looked across the bar at Jake. "Why you always breakin' his balls?" He stared Jake in the eye.

Jake shrugged, the smug look gone from his face. "I'm just messing around." He reached down behind the bar and came up with two bottles of beer, cracked the tops and put the bottles down in front of Louie and George. "On the house," he said as he wiped his hands on the towel draped over his shoulder.

Jake leaned on the bar again, this time with his elbows down, his head almost on top of George he was so close. He looked back and forth along the bar. "Victor Albanese was in here last night."

Louie gave George a quick glance. "So?"

"You must've heard his house got broken into? Stole a bunch of jewelry and one of his belts. The belt from his first Championship, I guess. They caught the guy—some ex-con—but I guess they still haven't found the belt." Jake straightened up off the bar. "Victor wants to kill the guy, he ever gets out."

"He's in jail?" George said. He assumed Jake didn't have the full story anyway.

Jake nodded. "Caught the guy right there in the driveway with his dick in his hands. I hear the guy was too drunk to make a run. No spring chicken, either... from what I hear."

Louie sipped his beer, held it up near his lips and said, "Victor told you this?"

Jake nodded again. "He said he had a camera on his house. Saw someone else run through the woods, but it was too dark to see the face or get any sort of ID."

George's heart raced. How the hell'd he miss a camera? But he tried to stay cool, sipped his beer and let Jake do all the talking. He felt Louie glance at him every few seconds, but kept his head straight ahead.

"Victor's getting up there in age, but I'm sure he still knows how to throw a good punch. In fact, I've seen him fight. This guy came in here one night, giving Victor some shit. I told them to take it outside. So they did. Victor came back in thirty-seconds later. I went outside, guy was out cold on the sidewalk... face all bloodied. Had to call the rescue."

Jake walked away from George and Louie as an older gentleman walked in, took a seat at the far end of the bar.

Louie turned to George. "So your friend... looks like he had some help."

George could feel Louie staring at him, but he sipped his beer, kept his eyes straight ahead. He didn't say a word to Louie.

He didn't have to.

17

GEORGE WAS ON the couch back at Louie's apartment when he finally turned on his phone and listened to a message Roy had left him.

It wasn't what George wanted to hear. There was background noise on the message. Bob Seeger's *Hollywood Nights* played, mixed with the distinct sound of glasses clinking... people talking. "George, it's Roy. I'm at the bar at Chopmist Hill Inn. Thought you'd want to know, this skinny guy came in, one of those flat caps on his head... was looking for you. Heard him ask the bartender if he knew where to find you."

George didn't even listen to the rest of the message, hung up and got up from the couch, walked to the window and looked down at the street. Cars were parked up and down along the sidewalk, and he ran his eyes along each one. He tried to remember how much he'd told Earl about Louie, other than when he mentioned him as the person who told him about the belts. Either way, he knew it was only a matter of time before Earl'd show up at Louie's apartment, looking for George.

He turned from the window, somewhat startled, when he heard the key in the door just off the kitchen.

Louie walked in holding a paper bag in his hand with something inside. He handed it to George.

"What's this?" George reached out and grabbed the bag from Louie.

"Protection."

George opened the top and stuck his hand inside. He pulled out a black pistol. "A gun?"

Louie nodded. "It's the Glock 45." He put a small box of bullets on the counter. "Just out of the box."

"From where?"

Louie tossed his keys on the counter and started down the hallway toward his bedroom. "Don't worry about it."

George stood alone in the kitchen and stared at the gun in his hand. The last thing he wanted to do was shoot someone. It wasn't his thing. But he knew Earl was looking for him and Earl was the type to shoot first, ask questions later.

No doubt about it.

He could understand Earl being upset with him. George left him all alone in Victor's house with the cops outside. But George didn't set him up. Why would Earl've even said that to Joyce?

George took a seat at the table in Louie's kitchen, looking over the Glock. When Louie said he'd get him a gun, he expected a Saturday Night Special from the hock shop. But the Glock was straight off the back of a truck. George was sure of it.

Louie walked back into the kitchen, buttoning his pants. "Nice piece, uh?"

George turned and looked up at him. "I wouldn't know a nice gun from a shitty one, to be honest."

Louie grabbed it from his hands. "You know how to use it?"

George stared up at Louie, but didn't answer.

Louie said, "I'll take that as a *no*. Maybe we can head out to the range, show you a thing or two. It's brand new, you know."

"I figured. Looks it."

"These Glocks just came out... won't see many like this out there yet."

George nodded, not particularly excited. But he knew having a gun wouldn't hurt. "Can't you just show me a thing or two, right here?"

Louie gave George a look, his face a bit twisted like he was annoyed with George. "Here's what I don't get. For a guy who knows how to pick any lock, skilled at cracking safes, can slip in-and-out of a bedroom with a bag filled of jewels while hubby and the wife are sleeping... I don't understand how you've gone this long without owning a gun."

George shrugged but didn't answer.

Louie reached in his shirt pocket, pulled a cigarette from his pack and stuck it in his mouth. He flipped the gun in his hand and turned the handle toward George. "Here, keep it somewhere safe. Let's grab something to eat."

Louie and George drove quiet for the first few miles. Louie smoked one cigarette after another. His car, as always, was filled with smoke.

George had his window down.

Louie said, "That'll only pull the smoke in your direction, you know."

"*What?*"

"The smoke," Louie said. "Keep your window up or else the smoke'll get pulled your way, goes all over the place."

"It already is all over the place. I can't breathe." George waved his hand back and forth in front of his face. "Maybe you should think about quitting. I don't know if you've read the side of the pack in a while, but there's this rumor going around they're actually bad for you."

Louie laughed. "A *lot* of things are bad for you. Most of the good stuff, in fact."

"You never thought about quitting?" George said.

Louie took a deep drag, blew a stream of smoke

out the window and turned to George. He paused a
moment, then slowly shook his head. "No. Not even
once."

George hadn't paid much attention to where they
were going when Louie turned onto Main Street, in
Pawtucket. "Where're we going?" he said.

"I told you, grab something to eat."

"I know... but what are we doing over here?"

Louie shrugged. "Thought we'd go by Zip's."

George didn't like that idea. "No, Louie. Not right
now. Can't we go somewhere else?"

Louie glanced at George. "I thought you liked
Zip's?"

"I just don't feel like it right now. Let's go
somewhere else."

Louie raised his eyebrows. "Come on. They got
good burgers. Besides, there's this broad in there—
Roy's in love with her—nice to look at. Makes the
food taste better."

Louie gripped the wheel with two hands and
turned into the parking lot. "Chick's got a boy's
name. Pat or something like that." He shook his
head. "But she ain't a boy... I can tell you that much."
He laughed, slapped George in the arm with the
back of his hand. "Roy stares at her... he creeps her
out, I'm sure."

George prayed Samantha wasn't working, although
even if she wasn't he had a feeling the aunt would be
in there. And it wasn't that he didn't want to see her,

either. It was that he didn't want her to see *him* hanging around with a guy like Louie.

Not that George was an angel.

Far from it.

But he was clean-cut and decent looking. The boy-next-door in his Sperry boat shoes and khaki shorts.

Louie, on the other hand, was what some might describe as a *spaccone*.

With his arm across the back of George's seat, he had his head turned and backed his car into a tight spot under the shade of an old maple tree. Whenever Louie parked, he never pulled straight in. He'd always back the car into a spot. He'd say 'Car's gotta be ready to go.'

George looked out the windshield at the diner. And toward the back of the building, just off a set of stairs, he noticed Samantha with a guy with his hair slicked back, his hands flailing all over the place.

Samantha was crying.

George put down the window and tried to listen

"What're you doing?" Louie said. "Put the window up."

George noticed the same Dodge Charger he saw her get in when she stood out front the other day. It was her ex-boyfriend's car.

George stepped from Louie's car without saying a word. He walked across the lot toward Samantha.

Louie said, "George? Where you goin'?"

George didn't answer.

Samantha looked right at George as he walked up behind the ex-boyfriend. She shook her head but George didn't pay it much attention.

The man turned. He was younger and smaller than George but tight muscles ran up and down his arms and into a thick neck that popped out from his too-tight tank top. He gave George a nod. "What the hell you looking at, bro?"

Samantha said, "Nick, don't..."

George stood between Nick and Samantha. "Is everything okay?" He looked into her eyes and knew she was scared.

But she didn't answer his question.

"Nick," George said. "Is that your name? Nick?"

Nick stared back at him. He clenched both fists.

"Let me ask one more time. Is everything all right over here?"

Louie walked up behind George and with his eyes on Sam. He smiled. "Hey, we were just talking about you!"

Nick took a step forward and got right up in George's face. "Why don't you and your boyfriend mind your own business?" He pushed out his chest and glared back at George. It was clear he wasn't afraid of the height advantage George had over him. Or the man advantage George had with Louie. "You hear me?" Nick said. "Move along, Chachi."

"Chachi?" Louie said. "Who the hell's Chachi?"

"Sam, why don't you go inside," George said.

Louie said, "Sam? That's right. Sam. I knew she had a boy's name."

Nick turned to Samantha. "Don't go anywhere."

George grabbed Nick by the shoulder to turn him around.

But as he did Nick came around with his fist flying and caught George right in the nose.

Sam screamed as blood poured down George's face. He tried to cover himself but another punch came over the top and hit him square in the back of the head.

George dove at Nick and wrapped both arms around his neck. But Nick kept the punches coming as one-jab-after-another landed in George's back.

Nick broke free of George's grasp, hit him right in the chin and sent him backward into Louie.

Louie reached into his pants and pulled out his gun. He pointed it at Nick and held it ten inches from the side of his head.

George came across with a punch and landed one on Nick's jaw. But Nick didn't budge as George grabbed his own hand in pain.

Louie stepped forward with his hand wrapped around his gun and struck Nick on the top of his head. He followed it again, swung his gun down on Nick and hit him three or four times.

Nick fell to his knees, holding the back of his head with both hands as blood dripped through his fingers and down the back of his shirt.

Sam screamed then covered her mouth with her hands as tears ran down her face.

The back door swung open and an old man with a chef's hat on his head swung a shotgun from his side. He pointed it at George and Louie and racked the slide.

Sam screamed and ran past him and through the same door the old man had just come out of.

"Get the hell off my goddamn property." The old man stepped down the stairs with the shotgun held straight out in front of him, moving the muzzle back and forth from George to Louie.

George wiped the blood from the side of his face, tried to explain. "This punk... he was bothering Sam, he was—"

The man held the muzzle high, pointed at George. He stood over Nick and yelled to George and Louie. *"I told you to get the hell off this property!"*

Louie grabbed George by the arm and pulled him across the lot.

They both got in Louie's car and took off as George looked back, watched the old man ease the shotgun down by his side. Nick was up on one knee, still holding the back of his head with both hands.

Louie ripped the wheel. The tires squealed as they jumped the curb and hit the street... fishtailed and drove full speed away from the diner. Without taking his eyes from the road, he said, "So I take it you've met Sam?"

18

LOUIE PULLED INTO the Burger King parking lot and cut over to the drive through lane. He ordered two cheeseburgers, fries, and a soda. He glanced at George. "Getting anything?"

George leaned over from the passenger seat and tried to look past Louie, at the menu outside the driver's side door. "Same thing, I guess."

Louie pulled the car forward, paid the girl in the window with cash and sat quiet for a moment. He turned to George. "You gonna tell me why you didn't say you knew that girl?"

"Who, Sam?"

"Who the hell else would I be talking about?"

George shrugged. "What's the big deal? I've seen her in there a couple of times."

"You've seen her a couple of times? So it's no big deal you just decide to hop out of my car, pick a fight with the boyfriend... like you're the big hero, save the little lady?"

George straightened up in his seat. "You're the one who pistol whipped the kid."

Louie turned and reached for the two paper bags as the girl held them out the drive-through window. He reached inside one of the bags, grabbed a handful of fries and passed the other bag to George. "You know, if it wasn't for *me...*" Louie shook his head. "The kid was just gettin' started... you might not've made it out of that parking lot alive." He shoved the handful of fries in his mouth.

George reached inside the bag, pulled out a cheeseburger wrapped in wax paper and laid it on his lap. He took a bite of the burger, chewed it on one side and said, "I hope the old man didn't call the cops."

Louie drove toward the street with the white bag between his legs, a burger in one hand rested on the top of the steering wheel as he turned out onto the street. "Anything comes up, we were protecting the girl. Not even sure why the old man'd come out, point that thing at us without asking what's up, first." He took a bite of his burger, turned to George. "You been out, what, two... three weeks now?"

George sipped his soda from a straw so he could clear the clump of fries from his throat. "Four weeks, tomorrow."

Louie rolled out a slight laugh. "So much for laying low, huh?"

George stared back at him for a moment but didn't respond. "I'm trying to."

Louie raised his eyebrows on his head. "Trying to? Hasn't even been a month, you've been kicked off your sister's couch, got an ex-con hunting you down, and an old man with a shotgun was about to end it all for you." Louie shoved what was left of his cheeseburger in his mouth. "Now you gotta worry about this girl's boyfriend." He glanced at George. "You don't think he's going to let this go, do you." Louie's eyes moved up into the rearview. He stared in the mirror as he sipped his soda from the straw.

George looked at Louie and followed his eyes to the rearview. He turned toward the back window. "Oh, shit," he said as he straightened out in his seat, pulled the seatbelt across his body..

There was a cop's car behind them.

"Relax," Louie said as he moved his eyes back and forth from the road ahead to the rearview mirror.

"Relax?" George said. "We left a kid bloodied in the parking lot of Zip's Diner. They must've called."

Louie shrugged. "It was self defense." He kept his eyes up in the rearview, glanced at the speedometer and tapped his breaks. "His lights aren't on." He narrowed his eyes and leaned in closer toward the mirror. "No shit," he said. "It's not a *he*. It's your girlfriend."

"Dawn?" George didn't turn to look. He pointed to a parking lot on the right. "Pull in there, see if she follows."

Louie nodded as he cut the wheel and pulled into a parking lot, a sign at the entrance was covered in doctor's names and medical-type businesses, like *Alton Blood Labs* and *Luxor Dental.*

George slouched down and leaned toward the passenger door, trying to see out the side view mirror. "Is she behind us?"

Louie nodded.

He drove to the back of the lot, pulled into a parking space and put the car in park. He turned off the engine and pushed open his door. "Let's go. We'll tell her you have a doctor's appointment. Say you're dying... maybe she'll leave us alone."

Dawn parked her vehicle perpendicular to Louie's —blocked them in—and was already waiting outside her car as George and Louie stepped out.

Louie acted surprised. "Whoah, Dawn? Where did you come from?" He slapped George in the chest with the back of his hand and walked right in front of her. He said, "Look who it is, George. What a surprise... your old girlfriend." He nodded toward her and put on a big smile. "Been a long time, Officer Lane."

George leaned toward Louie. "Sergeant."

"Sergeant Lane? No shit, huh?" Louie nodded, as if he was impressed.

Dawn had her hands rested on her belt and narrowed her eyes as she stared at George's face.

"What happened?"

"George touched the bruise on his face where Nick had hit him more than once. "Oh, I fell... slipped on the step at Louie's."

Louie pointed with his thumb behind him, toward the building. "Would love to catch up, but we're late for an appointment."

Dawn narrowed her eyes, looked back and forth at George and Louie. "Are you sick?" She shifted her stance.

George tried to catch a doctor's name off the sign.

Louie was already ahead of him. "George has to get his prostate checked. Seeing Doctor Barbosa."

George glanced at Dawn, always loved the way she looked in her uniform. But she never appreciated it much when he'd tell her.

"Any chance you two were over at Zip's Diner about a half hour ago?"

Louie raised his eyebrows. "Zips?" He shook his head. "Haven't been over there in quite some time. Wish we'd thought of it instead of Burger King." He put his hand on his stomach.

Dawn nodded toward Louie's car. "Somebody reported two men in a car like this one. Jumped the curb leaving Zip's. Drove into oncoming traffic and cut off a whole line of cars."

Louie and George exchanged a look.

"That it?" Louie said. "Hope you catch 'em. But we gotta run... we're late for the appointment." He held his finger in the air. "Like I said, George is due for the digit."

"The *digit?*" Dawn said.

Louie nodded. "I told you... *a prostate exam.*" He gave Dawn a nod with his chin, turned and walked toward the building. He looked at George over his shoulder. "We're late."

Dawn glanced at the sign at the entrance. "Doctor Barbosa, huh? Maybe I'll wait out here for you, make sure everything's okay." She crossed her arms and gave George a look. "He'll never change," she said.

George shrugged, looked toward Louie standing at the entrance of the medical building.

"Does he really think anybody believes anything that comes out of his mouth?" She shook her head and got back in the cruiser without saying another word to George.

He watched her drive toward the exit out of the parking lot. She pulled out onto the street and disappeared.

Louie let go of the glass door at the entrance of the building and walked back toward George. "She gone?"

George nodded. "She's not an idiot, you know."

Louie shrugged. "I know. I was just playing with her. I wanted her to believe every word, I might've come up with something different. What man needs his ex-brother-in-law to drive him to a prostate exam?"

They both stepped back into Louie's car.

George reached in the white paper bag, pulled out his half-eaten cheeseburger as Louie started out of the parking space.

"Guess the old man didn't call the cops," Louie said.

"Maybe Sam told him not too."

"Or maybe that shotgun he's got isn't registered."

Louie turned onto Dyer Avenue from the parking lot of the medical building. He nodded toward a police cruiser parked in a Dunkin Donuts parking lot. "That her?"

George and Louie both watched Dawn, seated in her cruiser, as they drove past.

Neither one said a word for a few miles, until Louie finally turned to George. "So, how about you go ahead and admit you were at Victor's house when your friend broke in, stole that belt?" He turned back toward the front of the car with his eyes back on the road. "I don't know how many times I have to say it, but you can't bullshit a bullshitter."

Even though George knew Louie knew. And Louie knew George knew he knew... George kept quiet.

Louie lit a cigarette he had hanging from his mouth. "Okay, you're not going to talk? Then how about you tell me where you hid the belt?"

George took the plastic top off his soda, shook the cup and tipped it back to get some ice from the bottom. "They never give you enough soda," he said, as if he hadn't heard a word Louie said. "It's all ice."

Louie pulled onto route 6 and kept the wheel straight. He glanced back and forth from George to the highway ahead of them.

Finally, George spoke up. "We never got the belt. Not that night." He waited a moment. "I got it by myself... the night before."

Louie turned, his eyes wide and his eyebrows up high on his forehead. "You broke in? By yourself? When? Right after I told you about it?"

George shook his head. "I already knew about it. After I had a few drinks... drank half a bottle, took Joyce's car for a spin and ended up at Victor's house. It was in the middle of the night."

Louie shook his head, huffed out a laugh. "I don't get it. You're just about straight-as-an-arrow when you're sober, but you have a few drinks and you get a hair across your ass. You break into a place just 'cause you got a buzz?" He turned and looked at George. "It *is* a bit strange, you know that, don't you?"

19

GEORGE WALKED DOWN the far end of the kitchen at Frank's Pizza, went inside the walk-in cooler and came out with a block of cheese the weight and size of a cinder block.

Roy was standing there, waiting for him. "I've been looking for you," he said. "I went by Joyce's... she said she had no idea where you were." He paused a moment. "And that she didn't give a shit where you were."

George rolled his eyes. "I slept at Louie's. On the couch."

"How come you didn't ask to stay at my place?"

George shrugged. "I don't know. Didn't really think about it... just needed a place to crash." He reached down and pulled open one of the ovens, pulled out a sheet pan of baked eggplant and placed it on a cooling rack. When he turned from the oven, Roy was gone. "Roy?"

A moment later Roy walked back into the kitchen from the front part of the restaurant. "I thought you should know, there's some talking going on down at Keenan's."

George sprinkled parmesan cheese on top of the eggplant. "Oh yeah? Like what?"

"That guy, Earl, who got caught breaking into Victor Albanese's house... they said he's a friend of yours."

George kept working, walked to the stove and stirred the big pot of sauce with the long, wooden spoon. He kept his back to Roy. "Who's 'they?'"

"Guys at the bar." He watched George stir the sauce. "Is it true? You know him?"

He turned from the stove and wiped his hands on the apron tied at his waist. "We did time together."

"Why was he looking for you?"

George stared back at Roy, hesitated a moment. "Just do me a favor. Anybody asks... you have no idea if I know him or not. Got it?"

Roy stared back at George, his eyes narrowed a bit. "Is that how he knew to break in Victor's? Did you tell him?"

George shook his head, turned to the pot with his back to Roy. "I had nothing to do with him breaking in there. From what I hear, you weren't the only one that knew the house was empty."

"You weren't out with him? The night he broke in?"

"Roy, can we talk about this some other time? I got work to do. Frank'll be back any minute. You know how he is about you guys hanging back here when I'm trying to work."

George left work a little after nine. It was a slow night, so Frank sent him home early. And he didn't mind since he knew he had the apartment to himself.

Louie was out of town—down in New York—out to 'make a run' as he'd told George. He worked for a couple of Rhode Island associates' he'd dealt with on-and-off for a good ten years. But he never told George who they were or what he did for them.

He rode back to Louie's from work and leaned his bike against the side of the freestanding garage. Other than the light coming from the streetlights, it was dark as George walked up the backstairs to Louie's third-floor apartment.

As he got to the top step he pulled the key from his pocket and slid it in the lock. But the door slowly creaked open before he'd finished putting the key in the hole.

He was sure he locked it behind him when he left that morning.

The first thought was he'd wished he kept the Glock on him, like Louie'd told him to. But riding a bicycle with a gun tucked in the waist of your pants wasn't exactly comfortable.

He eased open the door the rest of the way and put one foot up on the threshold. He reached his hand inside on the wall and felt around for the light switch. He flipped it up and down. The light didn't come on.

He stood still for a moment, reached in and tried the light one more time, knowing the electrical system in the place wasn't exactly new. He knew Louie would have to go down to the basement once in a while, reset the breaker. Usually when he'd make toast or one of his girlfriends would use a hairdryer.

George's eyes had adjusted to the darkness as he stepped into the kitchen. The lights from the street shined in the window over the kitchen table and reflected off a bottle of beer left on the counter.

He was careful as he took each step and listened for any sounds from inside the apartment. He walked across the kitchen on the balls of his feet, the way he would when he'd first break in a home.

He reached up into the cabinet over the sink, where he'd put the Glock Louie gave him. As he felt around with his hand—he knew he left it there—he didn't feel a thing.

A voice came from the other room. "You looking for this?"

George stopped and closed the cabinet door.

He knew exactly who it was as he turned and stepped toward the open doorway to the living room.

Earl Christie sat in a winged-back chair and reached for the lamp on the table next to him. He turned the switch. A dim, orange light shined on Earl and lit up the area around him. He grabbed a drink from the table. His other hand held the Glock, rested flat on his thigh with the muzzle pointed toward the doorway, where George stood.

George hadn't said a word as he eyed a lightbulb and a bottle of Jim Beam on the table under the lamp.

Earl waved with the gun, gestured for George to move closer toward him. "Come on, George, have a seat." He nodded toward the couch with the white bed pillow and the folded blanket. "I'd say make yourself at home, but looks like you've already done that."

George didn't move from the doorway. "You hit my sister," he said, his eyes on Earl.

Earl wiggled the muzzle of the gun back and forth as he spoke. "She's got quite the mouth on her... that sister of yours. If I did do anything to hurt her—not that I did—I can't imagine I'd be the first to do so." Earl took a sip from his glass and stared back at George, his eyes narrowed for a moment.

"Now, George," he said, "how long you and I known each other? I personally saved your ass— more than once, I believe—going back at least, what, three years? Ain't that about right?"

George still hadn't moved from the doorway.

Earl said, "Now, maybe I'm mistaken. But I thought—again, maybe I'm wrong... I thought you and I were friends, George." He nodded with his chin. "Are you going to be the one to disappoint me? Tell me I been wrong about that?"

George hesitated a moment, his eyes on the Glock in Earl's hand. "I didn't leave you at that house. I called you, more than once. I yelled your name as soon as I saw the lights... I had no idea what you were doing. But I *told* you not to go upstairs. Do you remember that? But you didn't listen, no matter what I—"

"Shhhhh." Earl held his long finger up in front of his lips. He stared back at George and took a drink of bourbon. He looked at it through the side of the glass. "You know... Jim Beam ain't so bad." He put the glass down on the table next to him and leaned forward on the chair. He rested his elbows on his knees and looked down at the floor. He looked up at George and again waved the gun as he spoke. "Now, you gonna tell me where you hid that belt you took?"

George shook his head. "I didn't get the belt."

Earl narrowed his eyes. "Then why the cops keep asking me where it is?" He held his gaze on George for a moment. "I guess I don't understand why you'd lie to me, George."

"The belt that's missing is the one I took before we broke in." George shrugged. "Truth is, I'm not sure it's worth much money."

Earl leaned back in the chair and grabbed his glass. He put it up to his mouth, over the rim said, "So you some kind of expert now? You assume it ain't worth much, without askin' nobody who knows for sure?"

"I told you, my brother-in-law's the one... he knows the buyers. You name it, he's flipped it for cash."

Earl tipped his head back and finished whatever was left in the glass. "Louie, right? That your brother-in-law?"

George nodded toward Earl. "And that's his bourbon." He leaned against the doorway, looked down at the floor, thinking for a moment, then looked up at Earl. "So what is it you want from me?"

Earl put the gun and the empty glass down on the table next to him, leaned his head against the back of the chair and put his hands together on his stomach with his fingers interlocked. He stretched his long legs out in front of him. "Somehow, for some reason, the judge went easy on me. I was able to post bail. Maybe on account'a my good looks." He smiled. "I'll owe the bondsman a good amount of money. Money of which I don't have, as I'm sure you understand." He paused a moment, leaned toward the table and grabbed the bottle of Jim Beam. He filled his glass halfway. "I don't put all the blame on *you*. But I think we can agree... you played a role in my being in this particular predicament that

I'm going to have a difficult time getting out of."

"Earl, I already told you, I didn't—"

"I want you to help me out, George. And I'm not talking some rinky-dink score, either."

George was quiet, nodded toward the bottle on the table next to Earl. "You mind sharing some of that with me?" he said. "Not that it's yours to share, but..."

Earl raised his glass. "Of course. Go ahead, get yourself a glass... enjoy some fine Kentucky bourbon."

George turned and walked into the kitchen. He flipped the light switch—out of habit—and toward the other room said, "Did you really have to remove the lightbulb?"

"It's just theater, my friend." After a brief pause, Earl said, "In fact it's *all* theater, ain't it?"

George rolled his eyes as he grabbed the glass from the shelf, went back into the other room and held it out in front of Earl.

Earl poured the Jim Beam into George's glass.

"I'll be honest, Earl. I'm not sure either one of us can afford the risk right now."

Earl raised his eyebrows. "Risk?" He shook his head and laughed. "Tell me how this sounds, George." He sipped his bourbon, looked at the glass and smacked his lips. "I'll decide how much risk you can take, okay? That sound good to you?" He stared back at George, his look serious as death.

George held the glass at his chest, stepped back toward the doorway and leaned against the edge. "What's that supposed to mean?"

"It's supposed to mean exactly what I said. The only risk you need to worry about is the one you'd be taking if you don't help me out of my, as I said, *pre-dicament*."

George stood up from the doorway. "You don't have to keep threatening me, you know." His eyes went right to the Glock on the table.

"Well, I'd hate to see something happen to that crazy sister of yours... or that pretty little waitress you got your eye on over there at, what's it called, Zippie's Diner?"

George stood, practically frozen, shifting his glance from Earl to the gun.

Earl stood up from the chair, pulled on the waist of his pants and reached for the Glock... tucked it into his waistband. "How about I leave you to yourself, give you some time to think things through."

"You didn't tell me what you want me to do."

Earl walked past George and into the kitchen. The door creaked as he pulled it open and stepped outside. He disappeared down the backstairs without saying another word to George.

20

IT WAS AROUND four in the morning when George woke up on Louie's couch, looked down at his feet, still wearing his Sperry Topsiders.

He thought about that night... the night he got picked-off trying to steal a Harley Davidson. If it weren't for those shoes, he would've never gone away, never would've met Earl Christie... and wouldn't be laying on Louie's couch wondering how to get out of—as Earl called it—his predicament.

He remembered like it was yesterday. He'd already cased the house, knew the man was away on business. He was sure—but clearly not as sure as he wished he'd been—the man's wife and kids were fast asleep inside. It'd rained that evening. And as he'd rolled the Harley out of the garage he stepped with both feet in a deep puddle, the water soaked right through his beat-up Converse high tops. He spotted a pair of Sperrys right there on the farmer's porch, next to the front door where the husband must've left them.

He walked up onto the porch and as soon as he stepped one of the old boards creaked. He stopped, waited... then went ahead and grabbed the shoes and sat down on the top step.

He tossed off his converse and slipped on the Sperrys.

Perfect fit.

As he was about to get up he felt the hard, cold muzzle of what turned out to be a 12 gauge double barrel shotgun pressed up against the back of his head.

The wife kept it on him until the cops showed up... one of which happened to be his ex-girlfriend, Dawn. She read him his rights, looked down at his shoes, and didn't say another word.

He sat in the back of her cruiser with cuffs on his wrists and the back of his skull still intact.

Didn't end up with the Harley but instead walked out of prison three years later with the same Sperry Topsiders he walked in with.

George stood in the shower with both hands held up toward the shower head as he tried to block the cold water from hitting his body. He'd step out of the shower to wait until the water'd turn warm but it'd go cold again as soon as he stepped back in.

He wanted to call Louie, not only to tell him there was no hot water but let him know Earl Christie broke into his apartment, drank half a bottle of Jim Beam and walked out with the Glock Louie gave George.

He left Louie's apartment, but wasn't sure what to do about the lock Earl broke right off the casing on the door. He looked back into the apartment, but didn't think there was much else anyone would take.

He pulled the door closed and headed down the stairs and called Louie.

He answered on the first ring. "What's up, sunshine?"

"I guess I'll start with that there's no hot water."

"No? Shit, that's not good."

George said, "Is there someone I should call? Get it fixed?"

Louie was quiet for a moment. "Huh? No... no. Not unless you have a couple hundred bucks to pay the bill. Otherwise, you'll have to wait 'till I get back."

"When's that?"

"Tonight."

George thought for a moment, looked up toward the apartment from the bottom of the stairs.

Louie said, "You there?"

"Yeah, I'm here. Sorry."

"Is that all you called to tell me? There's no hot water?"

George hesitated a moment. "Earl showed up last night. Broke in your apartment. Was sitting there in your chair, waiting for me when I got back from work."

"No shit? He take anything?"

"Half the bottle of Jim Beam. And, well... he took the gun."

"The Glock I gave you?"

"Uh huh."

"Shit, George. That thing was brand new... right off the truck. Shit, why didn't you keep it with you?"

"Not when I'm riding my bike."

"What's that mean? You can't carry a gun on a bike?"

George didn't answer.

"Was it loaded?" Louie said.

"Wasn't it already?"

"Did *you* load it?"

"No."

"He take the bullets?"

"The box?"

"Yeah, the box I gave you."

George hadn't even thought to check. He headed back up the stairs to the apartment and pushed open the door. He wondered if he should brace it with something so the wind didn't blow it open while he was gone.

He walked across the kitchen and reached up to the top shelf of the cabinet. He pulled down the box of bullets. "Yeah," he said into the phone. "The box is still here... still sealed."

George felt like a moron, Earl had the upper hand on him with the Glock in his lap. But if George had known it wasn't loaded..."

He put the box back up on the shelf and walked back down the stairs . He grabbed his bike, the phone still up to his ear.

"So what happened?" Louie said. "With Earl?"

"I'll tell you more tonight, but more-or-less, he asked me to help him on a job. Although I guess he didn't really ask, but—"

"You don't partner up with a loose cannon like that. Next thing you know, you're doing twenty... got Earl as a cellmate. Maybe that's what he wants?"

"I might not have a choice." George walked his bike out toward the street. "He said he'd take it out on Joyce... even mentioned Samantha. Somehow he knows who she is."

"No shit, huh? He's been watching you," Louie said. "Threatened you with an unloaded gun. Can't be all that swift."

"I'm the one who sat there taking his shit... never crossed my mind it wasn't loaded."

George was outside Founders Square with a coffee, his mind going a mile-a-minute. He had no idea what

Earl had in mind, what he needed George to do for him.

There was no way George would do a bank—that wasn't his thing—and he knew a small, easy job wasn't worth the risk.

George was in his own world as his coffee cooled off. He'd been there fifteen minutes and hadn't even had a sip.

Someone said his name. "George?"

He turned and looked back at Samantha with a paper cup in her hand, the strings from her tea bags hanging over her fingers.

George jumped up from the table. "Samantha... hey, I'm sorry about what happened. I don't know what to say... I'm not like that at all. I guess I—"

"Mind if I have a seat?" She pulled out the chair across from him and sat down with her tea. "I'm sorry about my uncle," she said. "He didn't know what was going on... that you were trying to help."

"I'm the one who's sorry. I thought you were in trouble. Maybe I should learn to mind my own business. I overreacted and—"

"No, you didn't. I appreciate it." She sipped her tea.

"You're not mad?"

She shook her head. "My uncle had threatened to use that gun on Nick a few times. He's a bit overprotective, as you saw."

George felt a little more relaxed, finally took a sip

of coffee but it was barely warm. He laughed. "I thought I was going to get shot."

She looked back at George with her blue eyes. "I don't think he's ever even had it loaded or if it even works."

George kept quiet for a moment, his eyes on Samantha as she looked back at him over her cup.

He said, "You mind if I ask what it was all about?"

"You mean, what happened with Nick?"

George nodded.

She pulled her chair in closer to the table as the metal feet scraped along the cobblestone. "When I told you he was my ex-boyfriend, I wasn't being completely honest with you."

George waited a moment. "Oh?"

"I'd planned on breaking up with him when I told you that. So, I did. I broke up with him the night before."

"The night before we saw you out there with him?"

She nodded. "He threatened me... said he wouldn't allow me to leave him." She looked down at the table.

"He threatened you?"

She didn't respond right away, her eyes still down. But she looked up at George. "Yes."

George straightened himself out in the chair. "So, he deserved what he got."

Samantha looked past George for a moment but

didn't answer.

"Louie treats me like his little brother," George said.

"But you're almost twice his size."

George laughed. "He doesn't go looking for a fight, but he's more than happy to step into one if he feels his friends are in trouble. I guess he thought your boyfriend—*ex*-boyfriend—was about to get the best of me."

Sam stared back into George's eyes. "Just so you know, Nick's a boxer. At least he *was* a boxer."

George laughed. "In a strange way, that actually makes me feel better. He throws quite a punch."

21

GEORGE WALKED UP to Joyce's front door and knew—or at least hoped—she was still asleep after working third shift at the nursing home. He looked in the front window of the garage door and saw the step stool against the wall, just under the opening to the attic where he hid the championship belt.

He went around back and used his lock pick to get inside, which he did in under ten-seconds. He always counted in his head how long it took, and he'd come a long way since his uncle showed him how to do it when he was a kid. Back then, he thought a minute was fast.

He was careful not to make any noise, and slowly pushed the door open just enough so he could slip inside. He stepped in the garage and looked up at the board covering the access hole, pulled over the step stool and placed it just underneath. He, of course, would've preferred a ladder. But the stool did the job as he pulled himself up into the attic, just like he did the night he hid the belt up there.

He crouched down and kept his head low to avoid hitting the rafters. The attic was enough for storing a few boxes but otherwise it was pretty tight. He kneeled down next to the space between the joists and slipped his fingers under the plywood covering it. He pushed it aside and reached down into the insulation, even though he knew it might make his hands itch later. He didn't care.

But when he felt around, he couldn't locate the belt with just his hands. He pulled the insulation out from between the joists and felt nothing.

The belt was gone.

George's heart raced in his chest. He stood up and whacked the top of his head on the rafter but ignored the pain as he stepped toward the opening. He grabbed onto the framed edge and eased his body down out of the attic. He hung by his hands and with his feet felt for the top of the step stool. He looked down from the opening and noticed the stool wasn't there.

But Joyce was.

"You're lucky I don't shoot you for breaking in my house," she said. "I don't care if you're my brother, to be honest." She slid the stool under his feet and reached up to give him a hand.

George put his foot on the top step and jumped the rest of the way, down to the floor.

He brushed his hands together as he tried to get the itchy, fiberglass crystals off his skin.

Joyce held a shiny black gun, her hand hung down by her side.

"Where'd you get that?" George nodded toward the gun.

She held it loosely in her hand and waved it in front of George's face.

He pushed it away with his finger on the side of the muzzle.

"Louie got it for me," she said.

George nodded. "It's a Glock 45," he said.

She shrugged. "I don't know what the hell that even means." She scrunched her face. "What're you, some kind of a gun expert all of a sudden?"

George didn't respond. He wanted to ask her what she did with the belt. But he hesitated for a moment.

Joyce said, "I know you took that goddamn belt from Victor Albanese's house." She shook her head.

George opened his mouth to speak but nothing came out. He looked up toward the opening in the ceiling over his head. "I didn't mean to," he said. "It was just—"

Joyce laughed. "You didn't mean to take the belt? You should try telling that to the judge next time you get pinched. See how that goes over."

"I meant... I was, uh, impaired."

She rolled her eyes and shook her head. "You were drunk? Is that what you're trying to say?" She stepped toward the door to the house but stopped and turned back to George. "Why couldn't you be like every other drunk out there... get behind the wheel, go home and beat your girlfriend... get in fights at the bar?" She stared back at him. "No, you get drunk and can't help yourself. You break into houses... steal something just to fulfill some weird urge you have when—"

"I'm not a drunk," he said.

She put her hands on her hips. "Then why not just lay off the booze? Wouldn't that make sense?" She walked back into the house and left the door open behind her.

George folded up the step stool and leaned it up against the wall. He glanced up at the ceiling and realized he hadn't slid the board back over the hole. Joyce stuck her head through the doorway.

"I left the door open for a reason," she said. "You can get that later."

George knew something was up. She still had her bite, but nothing like it was most of the time. He stepped into the kitchen and closed the door behind him. He looked down at the table where Joyce was sitting and there it was.

She had the belt out in front of her. "You need to get this thing out of my house. I don't care what you do with it. Burn it. Throw it in a lake. Just get it out of here." She got up and leaned her back against the counter in front of the sink with her arms folded at her chest.

George sat down at the table, picked up the belt and looked it over. "How'd you know it was up there?"

She said, "Just get it out of here, please. I don't want anything to do with it." She stepped toward the table and sat down in the chair across from George. "What's it worth?"

George shrugged. "I'm not sure. Might not be much."

"Well then what the hell'd you take it for?"

George didn't respond to her. "Louie'll find out what it's worth."

"Shit," she said. "Louie's involved in this? I thought it was just you and that freak from prison."

George tapped his fingers on the table. "Actually, I was by myself." He grabbed the belt and stood up from the table. "But I might have to give it to Earl."

"Why would you do that?"

George shrugged. He didn't want to make Joyce nervous, telling her Earl threatened George and made it clear he might harm her if George didn't help him.

22

GEORGE WAS ON his bike with Victor's championship belt tucked inside his backpack. He felt himself relax a bit with a sense of calm that'd come over him. Maybe it was the fresh air. The quiet.

But it didn't last long.

He heard a car's engine roar from behind him, so he rode his bike up off the road and onto the sidewalk. He turned and looked over his shoulder as a car drove toward him, moving at a pretty good speed.

George stopped pedaling and stepped off his bike as he watched the car—a Dodge Charger—inch up next to him. The engine was loud and obnoxious.

He knew who it was right away.

Samantha's boyfriend, Nick, leaned over from the driver's seat toward the passenger window, his head stretched as he looked right at George. He said, "You and me got some unfinished business, my friend."

George stood still, not sure if he should lay down his bike and get ready or get on it and take off. "Hey man, I don't want any trouble."

Nick laughed. "Trouble, huh? *Nobody* wants trouble. But I think it's a little late for that, you know?"

George noticed the scabbed wounds on Nick's forehead, he assumed from Louie's gun.

Nick pulled the car off the road with two tires up on the grass in front of George. He stepped out of his car with his chest out and his arms dangling loose from his thick shoulders bulging out from his white tank top.

George laid his bike down in the grass. He pulled the backpack from his shoulder and reached in for the pry bar he kept inside.

Nick walked around the front of the car and up onto the sidewalk. He stepped toward George as he rolled his shoulders and whipped his neck back and forth... getting loose like a boxer who'd just stepped into the ring.

George stared back at Nick, still holding the backpack with one hand and the other inside with a good grip on the pry bar.

Nick put up his fists as he moved his feet back and forth and moved in a circle around George. He nodded toward the backpack. "Why don't you be a man, put that down and put your hands up... *mano a mano."*

George rolled his eyes as he tightened his grip on the pry bar and pulled it from the bag. But it hooked on the belt. George raised the pry bar from the bag and Victor's championship belt fell to the ground.

Nick and George both froze, stared down at the ground at the gold belt. The gold and diamonds and green and red stones sparkled in the sun.

Nick looked up at George. "Where the hell'd you get that?"

George shrugged. "I used to wrestle in college."

Nick's eyes narrowed. "That's my uncle's belt. You're the one who broke into his house. *You stole his belt.*"

"Wait a minute," George said. "Your uncle?"

Nick nodded. "Victor Albanese."

George's jaw dropped. *"Your uncle is Victor Albanese? The boxer?"*

Nick lunged toward George without answering and threw a wild punch at him.

George ducked and swung the pry bar as he came back up, caught Nick right under the chin.

Blood dripped down onto Nick's white tank top as he stumbled backward. He wiped the back of his hand across his chin and smudged blood on his cheek. He put his head down and charged at George like a bull, drove his head square into George's chest. With his arms wrapped tight around George's waist, he slammed him to the ground.

George probably outweighed Nick by at least eighty pounds, but it didn't matter.

Nick's hands moved fast as he sat on George's chest and threw one punch after another into George's face.

George tried to stretch his hand to grab the pry bar, but Nick kicked it away with his foot just as George's fingers were within reach. He grabbed hold of Nick's head, wrapped his arm around his neck and threw him on his back.

Nick landed next to the pry bar and reached behind his head to grab it.

They both jumped to their feet, Nick with the pry bar raised up over his head.

He was about to swing at George but must've followed George's eyes as he turned and looked over his shoulder at an oncoming car behind him.

An old, green Buick drove straight at them both, jumped the curb.

George dove out of the way but before Nick could make a move he was struck by the front of the car. He flipped over the hood and bounced off the windshield.

His body hit the ground with a thump.

George was down on one knee, his breathing heavy as he stared at Nick, facedown on the sidewalk with his feet hanging down into the street.

George looked into the Buick but couldn't see the driver through the smashed windshield. He had no idea who could've been behind the wheel.

The door opened.

Earl stepped out with his eyebrows high on his head and gave George a nod with his chin as he walked around the front of the car. He stood over Nick's body then shifted his look to George.

He looked around at George's bike and the belt and the duffle bag in the grass, then stepped toward the belt. He leaned over and picked it up, looked it over and turned back to George.

George stood up on his feet. "You killed him."

Earl shrugged, the belt still in his hand. "Did I?"

"Shit, Earl. What the hell are we supposed to—"

"Guess once again you were lucky to have me in the right place at the right time. Just like the first time we met." He crouched down next to Nick and put his hand on his throat. He looked up at George from the tops of his eyes. "From what I saw, this boy was about to get the best of you. Wasn't for me, it woulda been you, down on the ground like that."

George ran his hand through his hair and held it there, his eyes bugged from his head.

"You actin' like you never seen a dead man." Earl looked down on the ground and saw the pry bar, picked it up and walked to the trunk. He popped the lid and threw the pry bar inside. "Let's get him in before someone comes around that corner."

George didn't move. It was as if he couldn't.

Earl said, "You want to spend the rest of your life

in the can?" He stepped toward Nick and grabbed his feet. He nodded with his chin. "Go on, George, grab his arms."

George walked over and did as Earl said, helped lift Nick from the ground and carried him toward the back of the car.

"He's a lightweight, uh?" Earl smiled.

They lifted him up over the bumper and into the trunk. Earl slammed the lid closed.

George turned, looked toward the Dodge Charger. "What about the car?"

Earl said, "Guess we take it, no?" He looked over his roof toward the Charger. "Better than this one, but maybe wouldn't make the most sense... get pulled over driving someone else's car, got the man's body in the trunk."

George seemed to agree. "Then maybe we just leave it."

Earl opened the driver's side door and had one foot inside, his right elbow resting on the roof as he nodded toward the blood on the sidewalk. "That your blood?"

George felt his face, looked at his fingers then looked himself up and down. He shook his head. "I don't think so."

Earl paused a moment and shrugged. "Maybe you coulda handled him yourself after all." He stepped into the Buick and closed the door. He leaned toward the passenger side and yelled out the window toward George. "Come on, you gettin' in?"

George hesitated, looked back and forth from the Dodge Charger to his bike. He picked up the duffle bag and lifted his bike from the grass. "I can't leave my bike."

Earl yelled toward the passenger window. "You and that goddamn bike... riding all around like a goddamn school girl." He straightened himself out, his wrist rested on the top of the steering wheel. He turned the key in the ignition and started the car as he shook his head and rolled his eyes. "See if it'll fit in back. And make sure you don't leave nothin' else out there."

George stuck his head in the open window on the passenger side. "Where's the belt?"

"I got it, just get in." Earl shifted the car into drive as George shoved the bike in the back seat. "Shit," he said. "How the hell am I supposed to see out the windshield, all busted up like this?"

23

EARL BACKED THE Buick up in front of the garage door outside Louie's apartment, ignoring the sign taped to the window with browned masking tape.

It read: *DO NOT BLOCK GARAGE DOOR.*

Earl left no more than four inches between the trunk and the garage door as he shifted the car into park and turned to George. "Be sure nobody'll go near that trunk."

They both stepped from the Buick and walked up the backstairs to Louie's and stood outside the door. It'd been repaired since Earl broke in the first time he showed up.

Earl said, "I hope your brother-in-law's not upset about the door."

George walked into the kitchen and turned to Earl, still looking over the repair work on the door. "Give him back that Glock, I'd say there's a chance he'll forget about the door."

Earl walked over to the refrigerator and pulled it open. He leaned down and with his head inside, he said, "I don't have the gun no more." He turned and looked at George over his shoulder. "How do you think I got the car?"

"I thought you stole it."

Earl straightened up and turned to George with the refrigerator door still open. "I said it was *stolen*. I didn't say *I* stole it." Earl reached back inside and pulled out a Rolling Rock, cracked the cap and took a sip. He shrugged as he gave George a look with the bottle up to his mouth. "Traded the gun for it."

George put his hands on his hips. "You traded Louie's gun for that piece of shit?"

"It wasn't a piece of shit 'til I hit the piece of shit who's in the trunk... messed it all up." Earl lifted his shirt, exposed a small pistol tucked in his waistband. "Got me a better one. An old Ed Brown, 1911." He pulled it from his pants and looked it over. "Now this's a *real* gun."

George leaned his back against the counter, folded his arms at his chest and looked down toward the floor. "We gotta get rid of that body. We can't just leave him out there. And I guarantee Louie'll want no part of having it anywhere near this place."

Earl was calm and cool as he sipped his Rolling Rock. "After dark, we'll take care of it. Bury it way out somewhere nobody'll find it. At least for a while."

"Earl, we can't wait all day. I'm telling you, Louie gets home and—"

"You shittin me? Is this the first person you ever killed?"

George straightened himself from the counter, tilted his head a bit with his eyes on Earl. "*I* killed him? *Are you kidding me?* You showed up, drove right into him with your car."

Earl shook his head. "Ain't my car." He shrugged. "Besides, he looked all bloody to me before I even showed up. Looked to me, he mighta already been dead."

"He was standing on his own two feet, Earl. What the hell are you talking about?" George had no interest in killing people. He didn't even like guns. But if he had one in his hand right then...

The door swung open as Louie walked into the kitchen, took one look at Earl and pulled his gun from his pants. He turned it toward Earl. "Who the hell are you?"

Earl eased the bottle of Rolling Rock down from his lips, pointed with the neck toward Louie as he looked at George. "This him?"

George nodded. "Louie, this is Earl. Earl, Louie."

Louie had the gun down by his side, stared right at Earl and said to George, "What the hell's he doing in here?"

George went on to tell Louie what had happened

with Nick and how Earl showed up and hit him with the car as Nick was about to crack George with the pry bar.

Louie said to Earl, "You just *happened* to be driving by?"

"Sometimes that's how things go," Earl said.

Louie held his gaze on Earl for a moment, then slowly turned to George. "So where is he now?"

"Nick?"

"Yes, Nick. Where the hell's the body?"

George hesitated a moment, looked toward the door. "In the trunk of that green Buick down there."

"Oh shit, are you serious?" Louie tucked his gun back into his waistband and looked out the window in the kitchen overlooking the driveway. "Landlord doesn't want anyone blocking the garage."

Earl said, "Only place I could find, prevent someone from going by, taking a peek inside." He looked up at the clock on the wall. "Starts to stink, the sun gets to it. Thought it'd be better in the shade... unless you have a better idea?"

Louie turned from the window and looked at George. "I don't know what you have going on with that girl over at the restaurant, but she or the uncle ends up talking to the cops about what happened."

Earl moved his hands up and down, palms facing toward the ground. "Take it easy. We'll take care of them." He tipped his head back and finished what was left of his Rolling Rock. He made an "Ahhhhh," sound when he was done and left the bottle right there on the counter.

Louie and George exchanged a look.

George said, "No, Earl. You're not going to take care of anyone but the kid in the back of your car. I'll deal with Samantha and her uncle."

Earl said, "What, you're gonna tell her you had nothing to do with it when she asks? Hope she believes you 'cause you had a cup of coffee with her?"

"He's right," Louie said. "As soon as she finds out something happened, it's me and you on her mind."

"She doesn't know a thing right now, so let's just worry about that when we get to it."

Earl scratched the top of his head, squinted his eyes like he was trying to think. "Maybe we should have taken that Charger instead'a leaving it there."

"Too late at this point," George said.

Earl shrugged. "But I'm telling you, someone's going to have to deal with the waitress sooner than later."

It was after eleven, pitch black outside with Earl behind the wheel of the Buick. George sat next to him in the passenger seat and Louie right behind George in the back seat. They drove out from the city and into the rural areas out west, toward a town called Boxerville.

Earl laughed as they passed the sign once they entered the town. He kept his eyes on the dark road ahead. "Boxerville? You said this kid was a boxer, didn't you?"

George turned and glanced at Louie in the back seat. Neither laughed.

Besides the main street that went through the small village in the center of town, Boxerville was mostly back roads and dirt roads and a lot of trees surrounding houses you could barely see in the dark.

Louie said, "Why don't we just toss him off the cliffs they got out there, over the lake where the kids go swimming. They find his body, they might just assume he was out for a walk, slipped on the wet rocks."

Earl looked at Louie in the rearview mirror, the whites of his eyes the only thing you could see.

"Turn here," George said as he pointed to a road.

Earl said, "If George hadn't left the kid's car, we could've taken it out here, put him in the driver's seat, slip it in drive and..."

George stared at Earl and narrowed his eyes. "Goddamn it, Earl. You're the one that killed him. You should've taken his car, left this piece of shit behind." George's eyes shifted down as Earl moved his right hand from the steering wheel, put it on top of his gun on the seat between them.

Earl lifted his Ed Brown 1911, pointed it right at George. "How about you wipe that sentence—who killed who—from those lips of yours, before it becomes some kind of a habit, go around telling someone I killed a man. I oughta just toss you off that cliff with the kid... you don't shut that mouth of yours."

Louie leaned forward from the back seat and put the muzzle of his Glock against the back of Earl's head, "You put that goddamn thing away before I'm the only one in a moving car with a pulse."

Earl glanced at George, looked back at Louie with his big, white eyes in the rearview mirror. He laid the gun down on the seat and put both hands up on the steering wheel. "This man owes me for saving his ass, and now he's—"

"*Look out!*" George yelled as he braced himself with both hands against the dashboard.

Earl ripped the wheel to avoid a deer—a full-grown buck—right there in the middle of the road playing chicken with the Buick.

The deer won.

The side of the car clipped not one but two trees as Earl tried to avoid the damn thing, like a statue in the middle of the road. He ripped the wheel left to right and left to right as he tried to get the car under control. Rocks and stones and dirt pinged and banged against the undercarriage.

Earl cut the wheel away from the woods but the car slid, sideways, into another tree and bounced them back out into the middle of the road.

Earl slammed on the brakes and stopped the car.

They were turned in the other direction. Dust surrounded them, the high beams from the headlights barely cutting through the thick, dirty air.

"Shit," Louie said as he put his hand on his head. "My fucking head."

George turned, looked at Louie, glanced at Earl, then tried to open the door to get out, but it was the side of the car that'd smashed into the trees. He pulled the handle and drove his shoulder hard into the door. It opened. He put both feet outside on the ground and stared out into the woods.

Nobody said a word.

There was a loud thump.

George turned and looked over his shoulder toward the back of the car.

"What the hell was that?" Louie said. He turned in his seat and looked toward the rear window.

Earl grabbed the gun from the seat and pushed open the driver side door. He stepped out with his gun by his side.

George stood up from the passenger seat and looked across the roof at Earl.

They heard it again. Another thump, but louder.

Earl's eyebrows went high on his head. He looked toward the rear of the car then ducked back inside and pulled the keys from the ignition.

Louie got out from the back seat. "That come from the trunk?"

Earl walked to the trunk and put his finger up to his lips as he slid the key in the lock.

The trunk's lid flew open and Nick came up with George's pry bar in his hand. With one quick swing he caught Earl right in the side of the head.

Earl stumbled backward with his arms limp by his side. His eyes turned white as his eyeballs rolled like a slot machine. His body crumbled to the ground.

Nick jumped from the trunk swinging the pry bar like a wild man. He turned and took a good swing at Louie. But Louie ducked low, came up and hit Nick right in the balls with his fist.

Nick bent over and screamed in pain then threw the pry bar and hit Louie in the head. Before Louie or George could do anything, Nick turned and ran straight into the woods and disappeared into the darkness.

24

GEORGE WAS BEHIND the wheel of the Buick, Earl in the passenger seat with a stack of napkins on the side of his head, trying to stop the bleeding.

Louie sat in back, blood dripping from his forehead. He didn't seem to be too worried about it. "It'll stop at some point."

George had his eyes on the road, jumped on 295.

From the back seat, Louie said, "I don't understand why you'd open the trunk, not have a weapon ready."

Earl turned in his seat, looked back at Louie. "Then why didn't *you* go first? Open the damn trunk... you knew how it shoulda been done."

Louie stared back at him. "You had the keys." He leaned forward against the front seat, ducked his head down so he could see himself in the mirror. He touched the wound on his head, looked at his bloody fingers. "Kid hit me with the tire iron."

George looked up at Louie through the rearview. "That was my cat's claw."

"What the hell's a cat's claw?"

"It's a pry bar, but it's got a rounded top, sharp hook on the end. Like a cat's paw."

"I thought you said 'cat's claw.' "

"I did."

"You said 'cat's paw.' "

"Same thing," George said.

Earl had his eyes out the passenger window. "Who gives a shit what it's called." He turned, looked at George and Louie. "We gotta find that son of a bitch. Why're we even leaving? We should be looking for him."

Louie said, "How the hell you expect us to find him? All those woods... it's the middle of the night."

Earl turned to George. "How the hell's he even alive? You said he was dead... didn't you check his pulse?"

George shook his head. "I thought you did. You're the one, reached down and grabbed his throat."

Earl shrugged. "What, I look like a fucking *doctor*?"

George looked in the rearview, saw Louie touch the gash on the side of his head.

Louie looked around the back seat. "My smokes up there?"

George and Earl both shook their heads at the same time, but neither one looked.

George thought for a moment, scratched his head

with his eyes still in the rearview, looking at Louie. "Hey, where's the cat's claw?"

Louie shrugged. "How should I know?" He padded his pockets. "You sure my cigarettes aren't up there?"

"Louie, I'm serious. What'd you do with it?"

"The pry bar?"

"Yeah, after he threw it at you? Did you pick it up?"

Louie shook his head. "Didn't you?"

Earl watched Louie and George from the passenger seat. He said, "What's the problem?"

George had his eyes back on the road. "My cat's claw!"

"We'll get you another one," Earl said. "If it'll make you feel better."

"It's got my fingerprints on it. All our fingerprints. And Nick's blood, I'm sure... they trace it back to us and to Victor's house and—"

"I see what you're getting at," Earl said as he nodded slowly.

George turned to Earl. "We gotta go back." He ripped the wheel off the first exit he saw, jumped back on the highway and headed in the other direction toward Boxerville. He looked up in the rearview, saw Louie slumped down against the back seat.

Earl said, "We turn around, you mean the way you turned around when you left me at Victor's house with my pants down?"

Louie spoke up. "You gettin' pinched is nobody's fault but your own, from what I hear. You walk around with your head in your ass... you got what you deserved."

Earl turned, looked at Louie over his shoulder. "Who the hell's asking you?" He turned to George. "We gotta get rid of this car, you know...shit all over the trunk."

George shrugged. "And do what, walk the rest of the way?"

Earl shook his head. "No. But I got a friend... same guy gave me this one." He pointed with his finger toward the windshield. "Take the next exit."

George did as Earl said, followed his directions for the next few miles then pulled up to a brick building with a small parking lot just off the street. A chain hung across the entrance.

Earl said, "Stop here." He opened the passenger door and stepped out then unhooked the chain. He nodded his head to the side for George to drive through. He hooked up the chain then got back in the car and pointed toward the brick building with the garage door on the front. "Over there. Park in front."

George stopped a few feet in front of the building with the headlights shining off the garage door.

Earl got out, walked inside a door at the side of the garage and disappeared inside.

Louie leaned forward, his arms up on the back of George's seat. "We gotta lose this guy. He's bad news."

George turned, looked right at Louie. "What are *we?*"

Louie rolled his eyes. "I mean, I'm no Mother Theresa but, come on... this guy's a friggin' loose cannon. He's going to get us killed. Or worse."

"I don't help him, he'll go after Joyce. Even mentioned Samantha's name... he knows exactly who she is."

"Yeah? Is that what he said?" Louie leaned back again. "He killed the kid, didn't he? Why should *we* have to deal with it." He leaned forward and disappeared out of sight for a moment, came back up with a pack of cigarettes in his hand. "Here they are." He stuck one in his mouth, lifted himself up off the seat and pulled a lighter from his pocket.

George said, "We almost killed him ourselves, if you remember how this all started. You pistol-whipped him, could've killed him right there. If the old man didn't come out with that shotgun..."

Louie shrugged. "I did it to save your ass, now you're going to throw it back at me, like any of this is *my* fault?"

George shook his head, looked out the busted windshield toward the garage door.

Louie said, "Listen, you know we're not going to find this kid. I'm not sure it's worth driving out there, as if—"

"I don't see how we'll find him either. But that pry bar... it's all the cops need. Especially he doesn't make it, find his body somewhere out there."

They were both quiet for a few moments.

Louie said, "I hate to say it, George, but maybe you're going to need to disappear. You think about it, it's only a matter of time they put two-and-two together... place you in that house with this crazy son-of-a-bitch."

25

EARL SWAPPED OUT the green Buick with the smashed windshield and the dented hood for a Toyota Camry. He told George to get back in the passenger seat... he'd be all right to drive.

Earl squeezed his grip and turned his hands on the steering wheel, as if trying to break it in. "Give me an American car any day." He shook his head and under his breath, said, "Friggin' rice burner."

George stared out the passenger window, not saying much as Earl pulled the car away from the building and drove toward the street.

"All right, we got a new ride... let's go find the kid."

Louie leaned forward from the back seat. "I don't know how the hell you expect to find him in the middle of nowhere... pitch black outside." Louie took a drag from his cigarette then tossed it out the window. "I'm telling you, there's no chance."

Earl turned and looked at Louie over his shoulder.

"You got a better idea? We let that boy live another day... all three of us are goin' down."

George turned from the window. "You saying, we find him... we kill him?"

Earl didn't answer, kept his eyes on the road as they headed back out to Boxerville.

They turned down the same dark road four miles off the highway they were on a little more than an hour earlier. Everything was black with hardly any street lights except for maybe one every mile or two. There were houses scattered here and there, but Boxerville was mostly woods. In fact, it looked darker than it was before.

All three kept quiet for most of the ride until Louie spoke up from the back seat. "Watch out for the deer this time."

Earl gave him a look through the rearview.

George said, "You sure this is the same road?" He kept his eyes out the window. "I don't remember those trailers."

There was a long stretch of cleared land that appeared to be a mobile park. They passed a sign that said, *Thank You Jesus*, stuck in the grass in front of a small house that looked like it was ready to fall down.

Earl said, "Why the hell would someone living in a

shit hole like that thank Jesus?" He shook his head, then laughed with a high-pitched squeal George had only heard once or twice when they were in prison.

George kept his eyes on the woods, hoping they'd somehow get lucky. Not that he was one to pray, but he'd thank Jesus if somehow they found Nick.

Earl turned to George. "This whole area's one big-ass forest." He paused a moment. "Ain't there a park around here somewhere? We used to come out this way when we was kids, a big trip like we was on vacation or something. We'd go play in the lake, have us a good time... until we got a little older, realized we surrounded by nothin' but Swamp Yankees."

George said, "I had a dog who ran away out here when I was a kid. Someone found him, drowned in a pond."

Louie said, "Never even crossed my mind once to come all the way out here, in the middle of nowhere." He pulled another cigarette from his pack and stuck it in his mouth.

Earl glanced at George, tipped his head toward Louie in the back. "City folk," he said. He looked at Louie in the rearview. "Hard to find much nature in the city, ain't it?"

George sat up straight, turned his whole body toward the passenger window. "I'm pretty sure we were on the other side of these woods... a couple of miles from here."

Earl gave George a quick look. "Who are you,

Ranger Rick?"

"I'm telling you," George said, "this road loops all the way around. It's a big circle." He looked out toward the road. "We're on the wrong side. There were a bunch of big homes where we were before."

Earl shrugged. "Okay, no big deal. We just keep driving."

George shook his head. "You can't get all the way around. The bridge is down... road's been closed for ten years. It's still not open. At least I don't think it is."

"Jesus Christ," Louie said. "Been driving for how many miles, you're telling me we gotta go all the way in the other direction... just to find a goddamn pry bar?"

Earl said, "Unless he's dead, he can't stay in the woods forever."

Louie had his eyes out the window, toward the woods. "Maybe we come back in daylight, we'll have a better chance."

Earl kept driving along the road, going slow with his chin over the steering wheel. "So, you telling me I should turn around? We on the wrong—" Earl stopped, mid-sentence, as his eyes bugged out of his head. "Hole-E *shit.*" He straightened up in his seat, glanced at George and nodded toward the windshield.

Louie leaned up from the back seat and poked his head between the front seats. "This is unbelievable.

You gotta be kidding me."

Earl smiled. "Thank you, Jesus."

All three of them stared toward the windshield with their eyes on the road and what they saw right there in front of them.

Nick walked along the side of the road and didn't look back as Earl drove the Toyota toward him and then slowly pulled up next to Nick.

He turned and looked at the car. His face was bloodied and his eyes were lifeless.

Zombi-like.

Earl said, "The walking dead." He put down the passenger window next to George and held the gun across George's face and pointed it toward Nick. "Need a ride?"

George pushed Earl's arm down. "Put it away. He's barely alive."

Nick stared back at them with his mouth half open. Blood covered his face and his hair stuck up in all directions. He moved his mouth as if he wanted to speak but nothing came out. At least not right away. He closed his eyes and put up a hand, moving it back and forth. "Please... don't... shoot... me."

Earl raised the gun again toward Nick, his arm in George's face.

Again, George pushed his arm down. "Earl, put it away."

Earl cocked his head, his chin pulled into his neck. "You pulling my leg?"

George shook his head. "Not right here, Earl. Let's just get him... get him out of here."

Louie still had his head stuck between the two front seats. "Kid looks brain dead to me anyway... might go back to plan A, take him out to those cliffs."

George turned and looked at Louie. "Open your door. Let him in."

"You shittin' me?" Louie said.

George shook his head. "I'm not. Open your door, Louie."

Louie gave George a look. "I see what this is all about. You don't want the waitress to—"

George grabbed Earl's gun from his hand and turned it toward Louie. "Open the goddamn door, Louie."

Earl looked up in the rearview then turned and looked back over his shoulder at Nick. "You must be made of rubber or something, kid. Ain't never seen someone hit like that... messed up that Buick real good."

Louie had the gun in his lap with the barrel toward Nick. He stared out the window to his left on the driver's side, but glanced over at Nick every once in a while.

Earl had his eyes back up in the rearview mirror. "He still alive?"

Louie shrugged. "Looks to me he's brain dead. Hasn't said a word, has he?" Louie leaned in closer to Nick, his eyes just a foot or so from his face. "You there?"

Nick's eyes were open but it didn't look like anyone was home.

26

THEY GOT BACK to Louie's apartment and kept a pillowcase over Nick's head. They walked him into Louie's bedroom where they tied his hands with a long rope to the metal bed frame.

It was Earl's idea to put a TV on in the bedroom and turn up the volume. That way they didn't have to whisper and Nick wouldn't hear what they were saying.

George, Louie, and Earl stood around the kitchen, not saying much at first.

Louie said, "I don't want this kid in here. Especially not on my bed. You think I want his shit all over my sheets?"

Earl raised his hands up and down, gestured toward Louie to relax. He turned toward George. "So what about that belt?" He gave Louie a nod. "I hear you're the man to help cash it in, huh?"

Louie glanced at George then turned to Earl with

his eyes narrowed. "Help you cash it in? Help? It was my goddamn idea in the first place. As far as I'm concerned, this is between me and George. George went in and got it before you even showed up. All you did was steal some jewelry and got caught before you even made it out the door. You ask me? You get *shit* from that belt."

Earl said, "I'm talking about the belt George *didn't* get. The one down in that room in the basement at Victor's, locked up like it's the goddamn Mona Lisa."

"Why would we do that at this point?" Louie said. "We're in enough trouble already."

Earl shrugged. "We tell the uncle we got the kid. He wants to see him alive... he's gotta give us the belt."

George said, "I'm not sure they even get along."

Louie said, "Who?"

"Nick and Victor."

Earl walked to the refrigerator and pulled open the door. He leaned down inside and, with his back to George and Louie, said, "You ain't leaving us many options. Other than to plug the kid, get rid of him the way we'd planned." He pulled out a Rolling Rock bottle. "You let me shoot him out there in the woods, we'd be all done with this shit."

Louie gave George a look, turned to Earl and said, "Who said you could go in my fridge, drink my beer?"

Earl closed the door, popped the cap off the

bottle and let it land on the floor at his feet. He raised the bottle toward Louie without saying a word, took a sip and made the "*aahhhh*" sound once again. "You mind?"

Louie kept his eyes on Earl for a moment. He said, "George, what about the belt you have now? What's the plan? The thing is, I'm going to have trouble turning it over at this point. As soon as word gets out the kid's missing, nobody's gonna want to touch it. I'd be surprised I get a hundred bucks for it."

They both stood quiet, the only sound coming from the TV up loud in the bedroom where Nick was tied up.

George said, "What if we talk to Nick? If his feelings toward his uncle are really that bad... maybe we offer to give him a cut if we can work something out."

Louie and Earl both stared back at George.

"Wait, wait, *wait a minute*," Earl said, his long, boney finger sticking straight up in the air. "You telling me, we damn near kill the kid, tie him up to a bedpost after he stumbles in and out of the woods... you think the prick's going to all of a sudden want to help us out? Just for a little dough?"

"You got a better idea? It takes care of both problems... we don't have to kill Nick and we get cash for giving back the belt. Get Nick involved, maybe Victor'd be willing to pay for the belt."

Earl said, "So what's the reason behind throwing

in the nephew? We could just kill him, still get the uncle to pay for the belt."

George said, "I don't know about *you*, Earl, but I'd rather not have to kill someone if I can avoid it."

Earl sipped his beer. "You know if Victor even has cash? He ain't been in the ring in ten, fifteen years. A lot of 'em blow through all their dough, end up in the poorhouse."

Louie said, "Victor owns a landscaping company. That's where he makes his money now. Has a lot of connections, gets him big state contracts."

"So you're saying he's got the dough, might be willing to pay to get back a piece of his glory days?" Victor finished off the beer, put the bottle back down on the counter.

Louie reached up into the cabinet over to the stove and pulled down an unopened bottle of Jim Beam. He pulled down two glasses. "I'd offer you a drink, Earl, but you already drank my other bottle. Not to mention the beers you drank without asking."

Earl raised his eyebrows. "Yeah, but ain't we all friends now?" He winked at Louie.

Louie poured two glasses, held one in his hand and gave the other to George. After a brief moment, he handed his to Earl, pulled down another glass and poured himself a drink.

George sipped from his glass. "Anyone got any other ideas?"

Louie looked off for a moment but the expression

dropped from his face. He walked to the window and looked down toward the parking lot behind the apartment. "Somebody here?"

There was a knock at the door and they all seemed to panic, put down their glasses and moved around the kitchen without anyone reaching for the door.

"Who is it?" George said in a hushed voice.

Louie stretched his neck in front of the window. "Shit, it's Joyce."

"Joyce?" Earl said. "Your sister?"

Louie turned to Earl. "You might want to get out of here. She sees you with us..."

"Out of here? Where the hell you want me to go? She seems like an understanding woman," he said.

"You don't know my sister," George said. "Go hide somewhere."

"In the bedroom," Louie said as he walked toward the door.

There was another knock. From the other side of the door, Joyce said, "I can hear you idiots in there. Open the goddamn door."

Earl started down the hall toward the bedroom.

Louie said to Earl, "Make sure the kid puts the pillow case on his head, assuming he's still alive."

George and Louie looked at each other as the bedroom door opened and closed.

Louie opened the door off the kitchen. "Joyce?" He forced a smile. "What a surprise."

She looked right past Louie and nodded with her

chin toward George. "Your old girlfriend's been looking for you."

"Dawn?" George said.

Joyce nodded. "She showed up at my door, asked if I knew where you were."

Louie and George both leaned against the counter and glanced at each other.

"She say what she wanted?" George said.

"She didn't say much, other than she wanted to talk to you."

Joyce took her coat off and hung it on the back of one of the chairs at the kitchen table. She turned and looked down the hall toward Louie's bedroom. "What is that, your TV? Why the hell's it so damn loud?"

Louie shrugged, but didn't answer.

George said, "Was she alone?"

"Dawn?"

Louie said, "Who else would he be asking about?"

Joyce gave Louie a look, her eyes narrowed before she turned her gaze to George. "There was another cop in the car."

"In uniform?"

Joyce nodded. "Does this have something to do with that belt?" She shook her head. "I told you not to bring that goddamn thing in my house."

"I'm sure it's nothing," George said, although he didn't believe it himself.

Joyce again turned toward the bedroom. "Who's

back there?" She looked back and forth from George to Louie.

They both shook their heads but Joyce turned and started down the hall.

Louie jumped in front of her, his arms spread wide across the hall. "Okay, okay... I got a friend in there. A woman."

She stared him right in the eye, cracked a slight smile. "A hooker?"

Louie rolled his eyes and shook his head, his arms still up so Joyce couldn't get by. "You really think I have to pay for sex?" He looked past her at George —watching them from the kitchen—and put a half smile on his face. "Not since I was married to *you*."

Joyce lifted her knee right into Louie's crotch and dropped him down onto the hardwoods.

He grabbed himself with both hands, curled up on the floor like a little baby and looked up at Joyce.

She stepped over him, reached for the bedroom door and pushed it open.

Earl sat on a wooden kitchen chair in the corner. His eyes were on the TV—louder with the door open—but looked up at Joyce as she stood in the doorway.

Nick was on the floor with a pillow case on his head, his hands tied with a long rope attached to the bed frame.

27

GEORGE, LOUIE AND Earl leaned against the counter in the kitchen.

Louie lit another cigarette and took a drag. "We gotta get him out of here."

Joyce looked up at George and Louie from the kitchen table. "No matter what I do to get you both the hell out of my life, I always end up stepping in your shit. If it wasn't one of you, it was my father. Me and my mother... like we were cursed."

Nobody else said a word.

She had her eyes on George. "How far do you expect to get, hanging around with this prison rat?" She glanced at Earl and narrowed her eyes. "Man knocks your own sister down. And what do you do?" She shrugged as she shook her head. "You don't do *shit*."

Earl raised his eyebrows, twirled his finger next to his head and whistled as he looked at George. "She even tell you what actually happened?"

"I know what happened," George said as he straightened out off the counter. "She's right... you shouldn't even be up here. I don't know why I let you—"

Earl folded his arms at his chest with his eyes on George. "Why don't you go ahead, ask her what actually happened." Earl turned and gave Joyce a nod. "You gonna tell him how it actually went down, 'stead of making it out like you the victim?"

George and Louie both looked at Joyce.

She dropped her eyes toward the ground. "I told him to get out of my house. And he wouldn't listen."

George folded his arms and turned to Joyce. "You said he hit you. Isn't that right?"

Joyce didn't answer.

Earl took a step toward Joyce. "Go ahead, now. Tell these men what happened."

"He blocked my punch," she said.

"She came at me," Earl threw his arms in the air, waved them around like he was drowning, "swinging her arms like a crazy person." He tipped his head down and looked at George from the tops of his eyes. "Now, like I told you, your sister ain't all there." He glanced at Joyce. "All I did was put up my hands, you come jumpin' at me like a goddamn wild animal. You didn't fall into me like you did, you woulda hit the ground." He shook his head. "Shit... if I hit you, you gonna *know* I hit you." He looked back and forth from George to Louie, shaking his head with a look of disgust.

Louie ran his cigarette under the faucet and tossed it in the basket under the sink. He turned and said, "Listen, whatever happened, we're gonna have to put it on the back burner for now, deal with it later. First thing, Earl, is you gotta get that kid out of here. If Dawn's out looking for George, you can be sure she's going to stop by here."

"Dawn?" Earl said. "She the cop?"

Joyce put up her hand, like she was sitting in a classroom. "Uh, actually... I might've mentioned to her he might be here."

Louie threw his hands up in the air. "Jesus, Joyce! What the hell would you tell her that for?"

"I can't keep lying, just to cover his ass." She gave George a look. "And how was I supposed to know he kidnapped some random guy from—"

"Actually," Earl said. "We thought he was dead."

George said, "No, Joyce. Listen... I didn't mean for any of this to happen. It's not what it looks like."

Joyce shook her head, turned and looked through the doorway from the kitchen, toward the bedroom. She turned to George. "Is that what you'll tell the cops? You just happened to kidnap someone? But it was by accident? You really meant for him to be dead?" She stared back at George then turned for the door and pulled it open, about to step outside.

Earl pulled his gun from his pants, pointed it right

at Joyce's back. "Where you think you're going?"

George jumped between Joyce and the gun and put his hands up, his palms out toward Earl. "What the hell are you doing?"

Joyce stepped back inside and closed the door, stood behind George and glanced over his shoulder at Earl.

Earl slowly lowered it down by his side. He kept his stare on George, narrowed his eyes a bit then backed away. He turned and pulled a chair out from the table, spun it around and sat on it backwards with his chest against the backrest and his arms hanging down. He held the gun loose in one hand. "So, what, we let her walk out of here with those flappin' gums of hers? Like she's not gonna tell nobody we got a kid who's half dead back there in the bedroom?"

"We all need to relax a little here," Louie said. "Let's all take a deep breath." He grabbed his pack of cigarettes from the counter and pulled one out, stuck it in his mouth.

Joyce looked back and forth from Louie to George. "I don't want either of you in my life. You go on living the way you live, but just keep me out of it." She looked at Earl, kept her stare on him for a moment then reached for the knob on the door.

Earl stood from the chair and walked toward the door, pushed it closed with Joyce still hanging onto the knob. He grabbed her by the arm and pointed with his gun toward the table. "You sit your ass down. Nobody goes anywhere until we figure this shit out."

George glanced at Louie, watched him ease his hand toward the waist of his pants. He knew he had his Glock down there.

Joyce took a seat at the table, kept her mouth shut. She slammed the chair as she pulled it out from under the table and sat down, her eyes still on Earl.

Earl nodded and gave her a smile. "See? Nice and relaxed." He turned to George. "Maybe we order some pizza or something. My stomach's angry... maybe ease all our minds a bit, we get some food in there."

Earl turned for the door and turned the lock. He glanced over at Louie. "Was she like this when you two were married?" He shook his head and rolled his eyes.

George said, "I'm hungry, but we gotta get Nick out of here. Dawn or some other cop comes knocking on that door, we're all going down."

Earl looked at George with his back to Joyce, pointed at her with his thumb over his shoulder. "What do you say we bring him back to her house? Cops won't be going back there. Not right away."

Joyce grabbed a beer bottle off the table and threw it across the kitchen at Earl. But she missed and it smashed against the refrigerator behind him.

"*Woohoo.* What a woman," Earl said with his

eyebrows raised on his head. "What... a... woman." He held one hand on his stomach as he laughed.

But then all four of them froze, turned toward the hall when they heard a crash come from the bedroom. They were all quiet. The TV the only thing anyone could hear.

Louie pulled his gun from his pants.

Earl had his out already—locked and loaded—and walked ahead of Louie toward the bedroom. He got to the door and reached for the knob. He held his hand still for a moment as he looked back at Louie and George.

He nodded with his chin and pushed the door open.

A shot exploded with a flash from inside the dark room. Earl stood upright with his gun down by his side. He didn't turn or look at Louie or George but dropped his gun down to the floor. His body went limp as he fell to his knees, then collapsed against the bloodied wall behind him and slid down to the floor with his chin tucked in his chest. His eyes stayed open.

Louie backed away from Earl with his gun held out toward the door. The light from the TV shined from the room and projected onto Earl. The TV volume was still up high with a voiceover from a commercial for the drug Colago and how it prevents death from heart attacks.

Earl didn't go down from a heart attack. But he

did have a hole in his head.

Louie and George walked backwards all the way to the kitchen, Louie with his gun still pointed down the hall.

In a hushed voice, George said, "Where is he?"

Joyce poked her head out from behind the wall. "Is he dead?"

Neither answered or moved a muscle.

A shadow moved into the hall as Nick stepped out from the bedroom with a gun in his hand, pointed toward the kitchen.

Louie and George backed from the doorway and stood behind the wall in the kitchen.

George said, "He had a gun in there?"

Louie didn't answer but yelled to Nick from behind the wall. "Put that gun down," Louie said. "Let's talk this through."

George stood across from Louie on the other side of the wall and poked his head out as Nick tried to step over Earl's body.

But he must've caught his foot on Earl because he tumbled over and his head bounced off the floor.

Louie jumped out from behind the wall and held his Glock on Nick, down on the ground. "Put the gun down," he said, his arms straight out in front of him.

Nick looked up at Louie and pointed the gun.

"*Nick!*" George yelled from the other side of the wall. "This was all a mistake. None of this should've happened. Earl's dead. At least he looks like it... not that we haven't made that mistake before. *He's* the one who hit you with his car. Let's try and—"

Nick pulled the trigger but nothing happened. Just a click. He pulled it again. It clicked again.

Louie had his gun in his hand and walked toward Nick. He didn't pull the trigger.

Nick threw the gun across the floor and jumped to his feet as he charged toward Louie and tackled him down to the floor. They both crashed and Louie slid backward into the kitchen and took George down with them as he stepped in front of the doorway.

George fell and smashed his head on the edge of the counter behind him as Nick straddled Louie and tried to shake the gun free from his grip.

George pushed himself from the counter and jumped at Nick. He wrapped his arms around Nick's neck and tried to pull him off Louie, but Nick wouldn't let go. One hand started to fly up and down in a blur as he threw at least a half-dozen punches into Louie's bloodied face.

Louie didn't even put up a fight. He was limp as his head bounced up-and-down off the linoleum with each punch Nick threw at him.

Nick stopped and let go of Louie as he tried to pry George's arms from his neck. He choked and gagged until George finally threw him off Louie and flipped him on his back.

George jumped at Nick as the kid's feet kicked and

tried to move backward away from George, moving like a crab across the floor until his back was up against the wall.

But Nick swung his foot and caught George's leg, sent him down on his back in the doorway. Nick jumped to his feet before George could react, got on top of George with both hands around his throat.

George couldn't breath. He pulled at Nick's thick wrists as he tried to break free. But he couldn't.

George looked up and saw Joyce behind Nick as she stood with a bottle of Jim Beam raised up over her head. George let go of Nick and covered his face with his arms as Joyce drove the bottle of Jack down hard and fast and smashed it on Nick's head.

The grip Nick had on George's neck loosened as Nick's body went limp and fell right on top of George. Shattered glass and Jim Beam covered both of them.

George pushed Nick off of him and reached for Louie's gun on the floor, right next to Louie. He glanced at Louie's bloodied face and wondered if he was even alive. His own heavy breathing was all he could hear in his head, on top of the pounding pulse he felt in his ears. He rubbed his throat with one hand and held Louie's gun in the other as he looked down at Nick and Louie on the floor.

Both out cold.

Joyce leaned with one hand on the counter, her head hung as her shoulders moved up and down with each heavy breath. She gave George a look, her eyes wide open. She stared down at Nick. "Is he dead?"

"I don't know," he said. He slid the cartridge out of Louie's gun. It was empty. "It's not even loaded?" He looked back at Louie and saw his eyes were starting to open.

Joyce looked at George and shook her head. "Louie never liked a loaded gun in the house."

28

LOUIE WAS ON the phone making a call, holding a bag of frozen peas up against his left eye that'd been closed shut from Nick's fist.

George went down and got rope from the garage and tied Nick's wrists behind his back, ran duct tape around the rope and did the same to his ankles. Joyce helped him prop Nick up against the wall so his face was off the floor.

Joyce leaned over and looked down at Nick's bloody head. She turned to Louie, "Hey, you got any peroxide?"

Louie looked down at her but didn't answer. He walked into the other room, the phone still up against his ear.

George stood up after he made sure the tape was tight over the rope. He gave Nick a nod with his chin. "You're not going anywhere." He followed Louie into the other room, made sure he was okay.

Louie spoke into the phone. "Yeah, okay, Sal. I get it." He shook his head. "But we gotta take care of this today. The guy's blood'll soak right through the floor... shows up on the ceiling below me I'm up shit's creek." Louie was quiet for a moment. "Yes, I told you. He's already dead." He listened. "I have no idea if anyone heard the gunshot, but what's that matter to you?" He put his finger up to George, gestured for him to wait a moment. "Yeah, Sal. I'll do that." He hung up the phone and looked at George. "He won't come out here tonight. We'll have to clean it up ourselves. But we wait much longer, he's gonna start to stink."

George thought for a moment. "How about I call Roy?"

"What, have him come in... powerwash the place?"

"He's cleaned up crime scenes before, you know."

"Roy? No shit?"

George dialed the phone and stood in the doorway as Louie walked in the kitchen and stood over Nick. He said, "So where'd you get the gun? The one you shot Earl with?"

Nick took a moment, his eyes half shut with blood dried in his eyebrows. "Under your mattress."

Louie scratched his head, looked around the kitchen then walked past George through the doorway into the other room. He came right back in, held the bag of peas up against his face.

Joyce came in the kitchen with a towel in her hand,

kneeled down next to Nick and dabbed the towel on his head.

Nick said, "So, did all of you break into my uncle's house?"

Louie and George exchanged a look, but didn't answer him.

Joyce poured peroxide into the towel and blotted Nick's head.

Louie said to Nick, "What makes you think we had anything to do with that?"

George waited to open his mouth until Louie turned to him. As he did, George said, "He saw the belt. Right before Earl hit him with his car."

There was a knock at the door. George pulled open the shade. "It's Roy." He unlocked the door and pulled it open.

Roy walked into the kitchen with a small steam cleaner and a long hose rolled up and hung over his shoulder. He was dressed in a blue hazmat suit that looked like something you'd see in a nuclear facility, minus the big helmet. He had a suit like the one he had on, folded-up and tucked under his arm. He handed it to George. "Might want to put this on before we get started."

Roy looked down toward the floor where Joyce was picking pieces from the Jim Beam bottle from

Nick's head.

Roy turned and gave George a look. "I thought you said he was dead?"

George looked toward the hall. "Back there, in front of Louie's bedroom."

Roy again glanced at Nick. "Then who the hell is he?"

George and Louie exchange a look but neither answered.

George looked at the bag in his hand and turned to Louie. "You going to help?"

Louie had a cigarette in his mouth, held a wet cloth up against his eye. "You're the one who got us into this mess. You two can take care of it." He shrugged. "Besides, I can't see shit out of this eye."

George walked out of the kitchen and toward Earl's body. He looked back at Roy. "Come on."

Roy followed and stopped as soon as Earl was in sight. "Oh, shit. What a mess." He gave George a look. "You didn't put nothing under him?"

George nodded. "We used whatever we could find."

Roy turned and looked back toward the kitchen. "Does Louie know the neighbors?"

George shrugged and shook his head. "I have no idea. But can you help us out, or what?"

Roy looked Earl's body up and down, stepped around him and got a good look from the other side. He looked at George and nodded. "Yeah, as long as it didn't soak through." He bent over and got a closer look at Earl's head, down on the floor. "You shoulda kept him upright, stop him from emptying out like that."

"Clearly it's a little late for that. We just need to get him out of here, clean up what we can before anyone shows up."

"You expecting someone?" Roy said.

"Dawn was looking for me."

Roy held his stare on George for a moment. "You said on the phone you needed my help cleaning up. You didn't say I'd have to help dispose of the body. Because, if that's what I'm here for..."

"Roy, come on. Just help me out here, will you? I'll make sure you're taken care of."

He looked at George with his eyebrows raised, half a smile. "Taken care of? You got money all of a sudden?"

George looked toward the kitchen, caught a glimpse of Nick's feet, all tied up, covered with rope and duct tape. He stepped closer to Roy, looked back one more time. "That kid in there, on the floor? That's Nick Albanese."

"Who the hell's that?"

George waited a moment, looked down at Earl. "Victor's nephew."

Roy looked toward the kitchen. "Wait, that guy on the floor is Victor's nephew?" He took off his hat and rubbed the top of his head. "What the fuck did you guys do?"

"It's a long story. But if you can help us out, I'll tell you on the ride out."

Roy looked down at Earl. "So who shot this guy?" He leaned in closer to get a better look at Earl's face. "Wait a minute, this is the guy who was in Chopmist looking for you. He the one who got pinched breaking into Victor's?"

George nodded. "Nick shot him. But like I said... I'll tell you the whole story on the ride."

29

IT WAS AFTER two in the morning when Roy and George had Earl rolled up in a rug from Louie's living room and carried him down the backstairs. They put him in the back of Roy's van.

Louie somehow talked Joyce into taking Nick back to her house, knowing the last thing he needed was the cops showing up, still unsure anyone had heard the gunshot.

Roy was behind the wheel as he backed his van out of the driveway. He turned to George. "So, you going to tell me the story? Especially the part about why you never told me what happened at Victor's house?" He glanced over his shoulder at Earl inside the rolled rug. "I knew it was you with him, you know. The thing that pisses me off is I'm the one who told you about the place. Then you go in with this guy." He shook his head, his eyes ahead on the dark road. "You only called me 'cause you made a damn mess."

"Actually, Roy, if you want to know the truth, I went in myself in the middle of the night. A couple hours after you dropped me off, I told you I wouldn't do it. When Earl went in, I'd already been there the night before."

Roy scrunched his face, glanced at George as he turned off the road. "You serious?"

"Yeah, of course I'm serious. I'm sorry, Roy. I'd planned to tell you. But then, I don't know... I didn't know what the hell I was going to do with it. I sobered up, wished I hadn't done it in the first place. Stuck to what I'd told you... that I was done doing shit like this." George thought about telling Roy about the cash, but there wasn't enough there to split. At least, not any longer.

Roy gripped the top of the steering wheel with both hands but kept quiet.

George said, "Louie doesn't think the belt I took'll be worth much."

Roy huffed. "What's he, a boxing belt expert now?"

"Well, no. But you know he's the one involved in that end of the transaction." He shrugged. "Come on, Roy. He's the one who knows the people we need to—"

"He get it appraised already?" Roy said.

George shook his head. "No, not yet."

Roy nodded towards the road up ahead. "Is that

the turn?"

George looked down at a piece of paper in his hand. "Yeah, that's it. Make a right."

Roy turned down the small road he would've missed if he hadn't been paying attention. Roy stopped in front of a chain link fence gate.

"This is it," George said as he pulled out his phone. He dialed the number on the paper.

Someone answered on half-a-ring. "Yeah?"

"This is George. Louie's brother-in-law."

"Wait there." The person hung up.

Roy turned off the headlights and turned to George. "You call him your brother-in-law, but he's *not* your brother-in-law. He hasn't been married to Joyce for, what, five years?"

George slowly turned his gaze to Roy. "What? What the hell's that got to do with?"

"The way you act around him... you treat him like he's something special. Let him make all the calls, like he's the boss. He's just a two-bit crook, like the rest of us."

George shook his head and dropped his head in his hand and rubbed his temples. "Jesus Christ. He's hooking us up with his friend so we can get rid of the body. And you're going to sit here and complain about him? Or what I call him?"

Roy looked out the driver's side window, mumbled something George couldn't hear.

"What'd you say?" George said.

"I was just asking... why you and me're the ones to clean up the mess?"

Beams of light shined inside the van from the other side of the gate.

Two men walked toward them, each holding a flashlight.

One of them opened the gate as the other waved the flashlight, signaled for Roy and George to drive through.

Roy parked behind a Lincoln Navigator in front of a brick building with three garage doors. George and Roy stepped down from the van and looked around.

The two men walked up behind them.

George said. "Is Sal around?"

Neither one answered as they both walked past Roy and George and through a door to the right of the garage door. The last of the two to walk in the building stopped and held the door. With a nod toward the van, he said, "Let's go."

George and Roy followed them inside. The building was big and spacious and filled with dozens of cars—all makes and models—but most were stripped-down to the frames. There were a good handful of men working, either taking cars apart or putting them back together.

A short, plump man with white hair pulled back

tight into a ponytail walked toward them. He was well-dressed in slacks and a buttoned-down shirt with a silk-like shine to it. "I'm Sal," he said. He gave Roy and George a nod with the side of his head. "Follow me."

They walked into a small office with a desk and two chairs. Sal sat behind the desk. "Have a seat." He leaned forward with his hands folded in front of him. "So where is it?"

"Rolled up in the back of the van."

"Rolled up in *what?*"

"A rug. From Louie's living room."

Sal rolled his eyes. "That'll cost extra to clean, if he wants it back."

George and Roy gave each other a look.

Sal busted out a laugh, brushed his hand through the air at them. "Nah, I'm just shittin' ya," he said. But the smile disappeared from his face. "You got the twenty G's?"

George said, "Twenty grand?"

Sal looked past George and Roy toward the two men from outside, both standing just inside the doorway. "You met Two-By and Cement, yeah?"

George nodded, and assumed the man he referred to as Two-by was the tall, thin one. Cement was the other: short and round. He said, "Louie didn't say anything about twenty-grand. He said it was a favor."

Sal glanced past George at his two goons, who'd yet to say much of anything. Sal cocked his head back, buried his chin in the fat of his neck. "It *is* a favor. But that doesn't mean I'm doing this out of the goodness of my heart." He looked at Roy. "Kid, would you mind not staring at me like that?" He turned to George. "He's creeping me out."

George gave Roy a look and slapped him in the chest with the back of his hand.

"Okay, well... Sal, here's the thing," George said. "We don't have that kind of money."

George felt Roy's eye on him but didn't turn to look at him.

Sal leaned back in his chair and tossed his feet up on the desk. He put his hands behind his head. "So you don't have the money, but you still want me to do the work?" He shook his head. "I'm sorry, but it doesn't work that way." He sat up in the chair and pulled open a drawer. He pulled two phones out and put them on the desk as he glanced at one as he dialed into the other. He put the phone he dialed up to his ear. "Louie? It's Sal." Sal paused a moment. "Yeah, they're right here. No, not yet." He sat quiet, nodding. "Yeah, but, here's my question, Louie. Why'd you send them over here without any cash? You know the drill... it ain't your first rodeo."

Sal leaned forward on the desk with his elbows on top. He rested his face in the palm of his hand. "Okay, I see. I get that. I do. But, yes, C-O-D. Uh huh. Yes, but there'll be an additional fee. You understand, right?"

George and Roy watched Sal on the phone with Louie. They both jumped when they heard an explosion out in the shop. George turned toward the door, gave Two-By and Cement a look.

Neither one budged or even seemed to notice the explosion-like sound.

George glanced through a small window from Sal's office that overlooked the shop. He watched a man in a welder's mask pull open a steel door as flames poured out toward him. Two other men tossed what looked like car parts into the hole.

George turned back just as Sal put down the phone.

Sal waited a moment before he spoke. "Okay, looks like you guys are all set for now. I'm not a bank, however. So as I told Louie, the cost'll be twenty-five now."

"*Twenty-five?* I thought you said *twenty?*"

Sal didn't answer but nodded toward his two goons. His eyes shifted back to George. "Is it open?"

"The van?"

Sal nodded. "Yeah, the van. Can these guys get in there?"

Roy lifted himself up from the chair and reached in his pocket for the keys. He put them on the desk for Sal. "It should be open, but just in case..."

30

THIN STREAKS OF light snuck through the blinds from inside the house as George and Roy stepped up to Joyce's front door. As soon as George pushed the doorbell Joyce ripped open the door and yanked him by the arm and pulled him inside.

She looked out past Roy, let him in behind George and closed the door.

"Your girlfriend came by again. She didn't come to the door, but she was outside on the street."

"She's not my girlfriend."

Joyce rolled her eyes. "Okay, then your arresting officer. Is that better?"

George and Roy followed her out to the three-season patio.

Louie stood with his back to everyone else as he faced the darkness in the backyard. He took a quick glance over his shoulder but didn't say a word.

Nick was on the couch with his hands tied behind

his back. But his feet were free.

George looked down at an empty pizza box on the coffee table. "You ate?" he said. "Is there anything left?"

Nick looked up at George from the couch, but kept quiet.

"We had to eat," Joyce said as she smiled at Nick. "Nick was hungry."

"*Nick?*" George said. "Who gives a shit about Nick? I haven't eaten in three days."

Joyce shrugged. "You work at a restaurant."

George hadn't been to work in a couple of days. He'd already called Frank to let him know he'd be out for a few days. So Frank told him he'd need to give George's hours to another kid he hired and he might not have much work for him when he got back.

Louie turned from the screen. "So the two of us —the three of us, actually—were talking..."

George had his eyes on Louie but glanced at Joyce for a moment as she sat down on the couch next to Nick. She slid over and got close to him.

Joyce looked up at George. "He obviously didn't mean to shoot him."

Louie put his hand up to Joyce, a cigarette between his fingers. "Joyce, let me talk, will you?" Louie turned to George. "Nick's willing to make us a little deal. Help us out." Louie moved his hand around the room in a circle with his finger extended. "All of us."

"I hope it has to do with coming up with the money to pay Sal the twenty-grand," George said.

Roy piped in. "Twenty-five."

George nodded as he turned back to Louie. "Did Sal tell you it's twenty grand to dump Earl, plus an extra five for financing on short notice?"

Louie nodded. "Yeah, well, he don't just dump 'em. He's got an incinerator right there in his shop. You happen to see it?"

George looked at Louie and shrugged. "Either way, Nick's the one who shot Earl. That's gotta come out of his pocket. I'm certainly not going to pay for —"

"I know we got off to a bad start," Nick said as he straightened himself up on the couch and seemed to wince in pain. He cracked a slight smile, his eyes half-shut like he was stoned. "But I think we can work together." He nodded with his chin toward Louie. "That's what we talked about."

George looked back at Nick without saying a word. He glanced toward Joyce, watched her stare at Nick like he was a piece of meat. Not that Nick wasn't a good-looking guy. George could admit that. But Joyce was twice his age. What the hell was she thinking?

George shook his head. "Why should we trust him?"

Louie put his hands out in front of him, palms toward the floor as he raised them up and down.

"Relax," he said to George. "Just listen for a minute." Louie picked up a can of beer from the coffee table and took a sip. He turned to Joyce. "You got anything else to drink?"

She nodded toward the wet bar. "Got some Jim Beam, help yourself."

George watched Joyce. She acted strange. She still had the bite to her tone, but something was different. He said, "Joyce, can I talk to you for a moment? Alone?"

After a brief pause, she got up and followed George into the kitchen.

He turned and leaned against the sink with his arms folded in front of him. "Joyce, what the hell are you doing?"

"What am *I* doing?" She shrugged. "I'm trying to help you dig your way out of another hole you and that shit-head-ex-husband of mine got yourselves into."

"I mean Nick. You're acting like some horny old lady, the way you're in there next to him... hanging on him."

She glanced over her shoulder through the doorway and kept her voice low. "Why don't you shut the hell up, George? Who do you think you are?"

George ran his hand through his hair and closed his eyes. He pulled both hands down the side of his face, as if he could pull his own skin off with his bare hands. "He could put me—all of us—away for twenty years."

"You said it yourself, George. He's killed a man. It's not like he's done nothing wrong."

George shook his head. "We don't have evidence he did *shit*. That's over with. The body's gone. Nothing but ashes. The ball's in his court. So don't get your panties all wet... I don't know what we're going to have to do with him."

"You didn't even hear what Louie had to say? That thick skull of yours... maybe if you'd listen to someone else once in a while."

George and Joyce both stopped talking and turned to Roy as he walked into the kitchen, watching them.

"Sorry," Roy said. "Mind if I grab a beer out of the fridge?"

Joyce walked past Roy and out onto the screened-in porch.

Roy said, "I might go, after I have a beer. I haven't slept, and gotta do a job in a few hours."

George didn't say a word to Roy, walked out onto the porch with the rest of them. He looked over at Louie standing in front of Joyce on the couch. Nick had said something to Louie, but stopped when George walked in.

"Oh, please don't let me interrupt this beautiful bonding experience," George said.

"Christ, George." Louie shook his head. "I know it's been a long day. Or, a long night I guess. But you gotta try and be a little more open minded."

George poured himself a glass of Jim Beam, threw back a double-shot and turned to Louie. "Go ahead, tell me about this *grand plan*."

Louie took a breath and rolled his eyes at George. "Thank you for your attention." He tipped his head toward Nick. "He says Victor owes him money."

Nick looked up at George from the couch. "My uncle ruined my career. When he realized I could fight, and had—"

"A what, a punch like the kick of a mule?" George felt himself lighten up a bit, the Jim Beam going right to his head.

"He sabotaged my boxing career," Nick said.

George shrugged. "That it? Then I wouldn't *technically* say he owes you money." He turned to Louie. "Would you?"

"My uncle was *the man* in our family. The tough guy. *The champ.* Then he's like, I don't want this kid showing me up." Nick shook his head. "He didn't want no one else gettin' recognition, you know?"

"So what exactly did he do that he *owes* you?" George said.

"He stopped training me. Said I couldn't be trained... kept telling me I'd never be good enough. But I won every match against anyone they threw in the ring with me."

George thought for a moment. "So why didn't you just get another trainer?"

Nick shook his head. "Cause he knew everyone. Threw bullshit around about me, told every trainer he knew to stay away from me. Told everyone in the business I was too much trouble."

George glanced at Louie. "Maybe he was right?" He walked over to the wet bar and poured himself another Jim Beam. He took a sip. "So why would he cough up money, if we tell him we've got you hostage? Sounds to me like he doesn't like you very much."

Nick shook his head. "He knows he did me wrong. He knows he owes my family... they don't even talk to him anymore. I had something and he took it all away." Nick turned to Joyce, gave her a look. "You tell him he's gotta pay you. Whatever amount we need, he'll have to pay."

The room was quiet.

George glanced back at Roy standing in the doorway with a can of beer in his hand. He said to Nick, "Don't forget, you're twenty-five grand in the hole. You'll have to pay Sal out of your cut."

Louie said, "He thinks we'll get a lot more than that. He said Victor's never spent a dime on anything... got every penny he's ever made."

George shook his head. "I thought he blew it all?"

Nick said, "That's just what he wants people to think. He hides money all over the place. Even keeps a few grand in a little box under his bed."

31

GEORGE AND ROY followed Louie in the Toyota Earl picked up. They all agreed they should get rid of it, especially with Dawn snooping around. Nick drove in the car with Louie.

Roy glanced at George in the passenger seat. "I had no idea that when I told you about Victor Albanese, we'd ever end up in a mess like this. I thought maybe we'd grab some cash, walk out with a few grand and be done with it."

George stared straight ahead, his eyes on the dark morning sky with streaks of orange in the clouds as the sun started to come up. After a moment, he turned to Roy. "You know that girl you liked at Zip's Diner?"

"Samantha?" Roy nodded.

"You're not going to believe this, but Nick... he's her boyfriend. Or, I guess, *ex*-boyfriend."

Roy shot a look at George. "Her boyfriend? How

the hell could that guy be *her* boyfriend?" He said it like he didn't believe what George was saying. "Are you about to tell me this whole thing isn't just some kind of coincidence?"

George hesitated a moment, wondering how much he should even tell Roy. "It all happened when Louie and I went to Zip's to get something to eat." George shook his head and turned toward the passenger window. "I didn't even want to go there, to be honest. But Louie pulled in, parked the car in the far back corner of the lot."

"Under that big maple tree?" Roy said.

George nodded. "So as soon as I get out, I see Sam standing around the back of the building, you know, where the dumpster is? Right there on the corner?"

Roy nodded.

"Well, I see her and this guy—this kid—Nick. To me, it looked like he was kind of in her face. She's crying. I didn't even think about it, just walked over and asked if everything was okay. And next thing you know, Nick's throwing punches." George thought for a moment. "I'm not sure I remember who threw the first punch."

Roy kept his eyes on the road. "I'd guess it was him. You've *never* thrown the first punch, have you?"

George shrugged. "Doesn't matter, I guess. But, anyway... it gets a little crazy. He's got a punch like a mule—not that I've ever been kicked by a mule... but

I remember Mike Tyson said it once after he got beat by Buster Douglas. You remember that fight?"

Roy nodded. "We watched it together, didn't we?"

"I don't know. Maybe. So, anyway, the kid's got a punch. And I'm not doing so well in this so-called fight. Samantha's screaming... crying. I mean, I'm doing what I can to keep this kid off me, but—even though he's half my size—I'm just trying to keep my face from getting busted up."

George told him how Louie came out of nowhere and whacked Nick with his gun and knocked him down, all the blood coming down Nick's head. And then how Sam's uncle came out the back door with a shotgun in his hand...

"Why would you get involved like that? You don't even know her."

Roy followed Louie and Nick in the Toyota as they pulled into JJ's Furniture Warehouse, then pulled up next to Louie as he stopped the Toyota around the back of the building.

George put down the passenger side window and looked down at Louie. "This is good enough, no?"

Louie turned off the engine and stepped out as Nick got out from the passenger side. Louie tossed the keys underneath the Toyota and Nick limped behind him. They both got in the cargo area of the van and sat on a couple of milk crates behind Roy and George.

Roy put the van in drive and looked up in the

rearview mirror. "So, Nick, George said you're Samantha's boyfriend, huh?"

George turned and gave Roy a look. Why would Roy bring that up?

Roy pulled out onto the street but still had his eyes on Nick through the rearview. "Well? Is it true?"

Nick shrugged. "Why? You know her?"

"I used to go there a lot. George here was just telling me how you two met."

George stared out the passenger window, shaking his head.

"But you're not together anymore?" Roy said.

Nick didn't answer.

George stared back at Roy. "Will you just shut up and drive, Roy?"

"Why don't *you* shut up?" Roy said as his eyes shifted back to the road.

It crossed George's mind to throw a punch at Roy as he kept his stare on him from the side. "You're the only one talking, Roy. You need to just drive. I thought you had a job to get to?"

But Roy didn't stop. "I introduced Sam to George. So I guess you can blame me for what happened. You and George would've never had your little run-in, if I didn't take him to Zips. So maybe this whole thing is my fault."

Louie said, "Roy, George is right. You need to shut up and drive. We didn't go to Zips to see anyone. I wanted a goddamn burger."

"Yeah, but you should've seen Sam and George, when they first met."

"*What's your problem, Roy?*" George said, holding himself back from punching Roy right in the face. He couldn't figure out what had gotten into Roy.

"My problem?" Roy said. "Because I wouldn't have known any of this if you didn't need me to come clean up the mess you made. You would've taken the money and the belt from Victor's and cashed-in. Who knows what you all would've done with the money. But I'm sure I wouldn't have seen a dime of it."

Louie got up off the milk crate and squeezed Roy's shoulder from behind. "Roy, you gotta shut your mouth. Nobody wants to hear another word out of you. Just shut the fuck up, okay?"

Roy gave Louie a quick glance over his shoulder.

The four of them drove quiet for a handful of miles until Louie told Roy to pull into the 7-Eleven.

Louie pulled open the van's door and got out. He turned and stuck his head back inside. "Anyone got any cash?" He pulled a few bills out of his pocket and started counting.

Nobody answered him.

George said, "What's that in your hand?" George said as he hung his head outside the passenger window. "You look like you have cash right there."

"It's only twenty-five bucks. I need at least another ten."

Roy said, "What are you buying?"

"Phones. Burners."

George turned from the window and looked at Nick. "You have any money?"

Nick shook his head.

George turned back to Louie outside the passenger window. "You think maybe we should catch the news, first? We're driving around like we have nothing to worry about. But if they found Nick's car... they must know he's missing."

"Where's his car?" Louie said.

"Right where we left it, after Earl hit him."

Louie stepped to the back, sliding door and poked his head in at Nick. "Anybody care enough about you to be worried... call the cops?"

Nick just shrugged. "I don't know."

Roy turned and looked at Nick over his shoulder. "What about Sam?"

George gave Roy a look before he turned back toward Nick. "What about your parents? You must have a friend or two, worried about you, no?"

"Parents aren't around. My friends... it'd be a few days before they'd even notice."

"Okay," George said. "Well, I'm sure they find your car, the cops are going to suspect something's up."

Nick said, "Technically, it's not even mine."

"What's not?" Louie said. "The car?"

Nick nodded. "Yeah. I mean, it's mine—I paid for

it and everything—but it might've already been stolen. I didn't register it... the plates are from another car."

"From your car?" George said.

Nick shook his head. "No, they're stolen plates."

Louie shrugged. "Okay, then I guess that's a good thing. We have some time." He turned from the van and walked into the store.

George turned to Nick. "What about inside? You leave anything?"

"No, man," Nick said. "That's how you get caught stealing a car. I remember when I was a kid, my grandfather's car got stolen. The kid who took it was a DJ... dumb-ass left his business card on the front seat." Nick looked straight ahead toward the front of the van. "My grandfather loved that car. One of those nice Cadillacs with the brown, cloth roof. I don't think the kid ever spun another record."

Roy turned and looked back at Nick. "He killed him?"

Nick shook his head. "No, but my grandfather knew some people. I'm sure the kid lost a couple fingers."

Louie pulled open the back door of the van, stepped inside with a white, plastic 7-Eleven bag. He sat down on the milk crate and pulled out two phones. "Would rather have a couple more, use a different number for each call. But it is what it is. We'll make do." He gave Nick a nod with his chin.

"What's your uncle's number?"

Nick shook his head, mixed in with a shrug. "I have no idea."

32

LOUIE, GEORGE, AND Roy dropped Nick off at Joyce's house then headed back to get Louie's car from his apartment.

Roy was still in a foul mood. "I gotta stop and buy all new supplies before my next job. I used everything I had cleaning up that mess."

"So what? I gotta buy a new rug. But you hear me crying about it?" Louie stepped out of the van in front of the stairs to his apartment and slammed the door.

George got out from the back and Roy drove off without a word.

Louie headed up the stairs. "I gotta go up, take a leak."

George sat down on the lower step. "I'll wait here." He leaned forward, his elbows down on his thighs and his hands folded in front of him.

He thought he heard Louie say his name, turned

and looked up at Louie leaning over the railing. "George." He nodded out toward the street. "We got company."

George followed Louie's eyes to the police cruiser, parked no more than twenty yards away.

Dawn was behind the wheel.

Louie kept his voice hushed, but loud enough for George to hear. "Get rid of her." He slammed his door closed and left George to deal with it.

George got up from the step as Dawn pulled the cruiser into Louie's driveway. She left the engine running but stepped out and stood between the door and the driver's seat, her elbow rested on the roof. With a nod to George, she said, "Joyce tell you I was looking for you?"

"Joyce?" He shook his head. "Haven't talked to her in a few days."

"No?"

He stared back at her. "What, you don't believe me?"

Dawn didn't answer. "I was wondering if you'd like to tell me what you know about your friend, Earl Christie."

George took a moment, tried to play it cool. "What makes you think I'd know anything about him?"

"Just answer the question, George. You know he broke into Victor Albanese's house?"

George took a step closer to the car. "I heard."

"That's it?" she said. "You heard? You don't want to add anything else?"

"Like what?"

George wasn't exactly sure what she was getting at. Maybe she'd asked around the bar at Chopmist Hill Inn... heard he was in there looking for George. Or if she knew they had drinks together and George didn't admit to it... she would've known he was lying. His heart raced. But he wasn't about to give her more than he had to.

He turned and looked up at Louie's third-floor apartment, wondered if Louie'd come down or if he was waiting, watching them. The lights were all off. He turned back to Dawn. "So is this official business? I thought maybe it was a social stop."

Dawn let a huff out her nose. She said, "How about if I told you I'd keep it off the record... whatever you want to share with me?"

George laughed. "Why don't you just tell me what you're looking for? I haven't talked to Earl in quite some time, if that's what you're asking?"

"Have you seen him since he got out?"

He held his stare on her. "What are you trying to do?"

She looked off for a moment. "I'm trying hard to not always think the worst of you... give you the benefit of the doubt."

George hesitated a moment. "I guess I'll admit... I'm surprised to hear you say that."

"You shouldn't be. I can appreciate you trying to do the right thing with your life, if that's what you're really trying to do. But I'm skeptical. I've grown up a lot since you and I were together. We were just kids... I was naive then."

"What are you saying?"

"I hope both of us are capable of using our better judgement."

George waited a moment before he turned and started toward the stairs. He looked back at Dawn over his shoulder and said, "I hope you believe me. I have nothing to do with Earl Christie." He looked up at Louie's apartment and saw the curtains move inside the door.

"So, you're telling me you haven't seen Earl?"

George had one foot up on the bottom stair, looked back at Dawn. "That's what I'm telling you."

Dawn's eyes went up toward Louie's apartment. "What the hell's Louie doing up there?" She looked at George. "Is he up there alone?"

George nodded. "I'm sure he'd love to have you up for a cup of coffee, but..."

She walked toward George, went right past him and started up the stairs for Louie's apartment.

"What're you doing?" George said as he followed behind her up the stairs.

"Might as well say hi, while I'm here." She continued up the stairs ahead of George.

As soon as she was up past the second floor,

Louie opened the door at the top of the stairs and stepped outside. He pulled it shut and locked it with his back to Dawn, just as she stepped up behind him.

He turned to her with no more than a couple of feet between them. "Hey, Officer Dawn! What a surprise. Is there something I can help you with, officer?"

Dawn stood between Louie and George, George right behind her a few steps down. She had her hand on her belt; her pinkie tickled the snap on her holster.

Louie's eyes went right to the gun in her holster, then looked past her toward George. "I told you, George, one of these days she's going to shoot you... she ever gets the chance."

Dawn looked up toward Louie's door. "Anyone else in that apartment?"

He turned his shoulders and looked at the door. With his thumb he pointed behind him. "In *there*?" He shook his head. "Not that I'm aware of."

Dawn kept her stare on Louie for a moment, then turned and brushed past George as she headed down the stairs. Without looking back at them, she said, "I don't know what it is just yet. But I know you're up to something. And I'm going to find out."

Louie and George didn't move as they both stood at the top of the stairs and watched Dawn walk all the way down and out toward her cruiser.

She pulled open the door to her vehicle and looked up the stairs. "George, you hear anything about Earl Christie, I hope you'll do the right thing." She stepped in her car and closed the door.

George and Louie exchanged a look then watched her drive out toward the road. Louie took a couple of steps down and put his hand on George's shoulder. "Maybe I'm wrong, or a little pessimistic, but something tells me you and Dawn are never getting back together."

33

LOUIE AND GEORGE sat side-by-side at the bar in Keenan's, both with their eyes up on the TV.

Jake walked through the swinging door from the kitchen and put a plate with a burger and fries down on the bar in front of each of them.

Jake stood across from him and said, "This skinny dude came in looking for you a few nights ago."

George was about to take a bite of his burger, but held it down in front of him. "You get a name?"

Jake wiped his hands on a towel and shook his head. "I asked. All he said was he was an old friend."

Louie had a grip on his burger, chewed through it like he hadn't eaten in three weeks. He stopped and glanced at George out of the corner of his eye as he gulped back half a glass of beer.

George shrugged, looked past Jake toward the TV. "If it's important I'm sure whoever it was'll find me."

But for some reason Jake wouldn't let it go. "If a guy says he's a friend of yours, don't you think he would know how to get in touch with you?"

George washed down his burger with his beer. "I don't know what to tell you, Jake. I guess next time someone comes in looking for me, do us both a favor and get a name."

Jake paused a moment then turned and walked back through the swinging door and into the kitchen.

Louie leaned into George. "Last thing we need is this idiot chirping like he always does, helps make some connection between you and Earl. Dawn comes in here asking questions..."

George stuck a fry in his mouth and looked toward the door to the kitchen. "Dawn knows I was in prison with him. There doesn't have to be much more to the story." He grabbed another fry and dipped it in the ketchup. "Doesn't mean a thing that he was looking for me."

Louie wiped his mouth with a cocktail napkin. "All it takes is for this dope to start flapping his gums in front of the wrong person, brings attention to it... next thing you know cops are knocking on my door." He finished what was left in his glass and nodded toward George's empty plate. "You good?" Louie stood up, put a cigarette in his mouth and threw a few bills down on the bar. "Let's get the hell out of here."

Louie and George walked along the sidewalk to Louie's car when George stopped and looked down one of the side streets. He saw a kid—kind of a big kid—riding on a bicycle coming toward them.

"Hey," George said. *"That's my bike!"*

"Your bike?" Louie said as he stood next to George in the middle of the street, both of them watching the kid ride toward them.

"The one someone stole, outside Keenan's."

As the kid rode closer, George ran out toward him and put his hand up. *"Stop right there!"* he yelled.

But the kid tried to go around him. "Out of my way, asshole."

Louie stepped in front of the kid, grabbed him with both hands by the back of his shirt and pulled him down to the ground.

The bike kept going until it hit the curb and flipped up onto the sidewalk and crashed against a wired fence.

Louie held the kid down on the ground as George walked toward him. He grabbed the kid by the arm and lifted him to his feet. He pulled him toward him. "Where'd you get that bike?"

The kid said, "Get your hands off me, you freak."

George let go of his arm and grabbed him by the front of his shirt. He pulled him in toward him, his face close enough he could smell the kid's breath. George stared him right in the eye. "I'll call the cops, let them deal with it." But then George looked past him, saw the bike mangled and broken—the front wheel bent in the wrong direction—and eased up on the kid's shirt. "You start stealing bikes now... I know what comes next."

The kid pushed George's hand away. "Let go of me, you *weirdo*." He turned and ran down the street, cut across a parking lot and disappeared behind a building.

"What the hell was that all about?" Louie said.

George stood with his hands on his hips as he stared toward the direction where the kid had gone. He didn't answer Louie.

Louie said, "You want your bike? Grab it, throw it in the trunk." He walked away from George, continued down the sidewalk toward his car.

George picked up the bike, put the front wheel between his legs and straightened out the handle bars. He swung his leg over the seat. "I'll ride it home. I'll see you back there."

"You serious? You're going to ride your bike? We got things to do, you know."

George didn't pay much attention to Louie, started pedaling and took off down the street. "I'll meet you back at Joyce's."

Louie yelled, "*Come on, George. Where you going? Put the goddamn thing in the trunk and let's go.*"

George kept riding as if he didn't hear a thing, turned down a side street and didn't look back for Louie.

George sat on a bench at the park, the same bench he'd been on when he first saw Samantha out for her run. A lot had happened since then, and he hoped he'd see her again.

He only rode a couple of miles and already felt out of breath. His body was tired, as was his brain. But he was happy to be outside, happy to be out with his bike again. He liked being alone, and wondered how he ended up right back where he started. He swore he wouldn't go back to hanging around Louie and Roy and even Joyce. He knew if he had, he'd be right back in trouble. Even when he was in prison, he didn't think of them at all.

It's not like they ever went to visit him, either.

George looked up from the bench and first noticed her long, red hair as she ran past him.

He stood up, grabbed his bike, and peddled after her. "*Sam!*" he yelled as he tried to catch her.

It seemed at first like she'd picked up her pace. He wondered if she saw him, maybe tried to ignore him.

But then she turned, glanced over her shoulder and looked right at him. She pulled the earbuds from her ears and jogged off to the edge of the path. Her breathing was heavy.

George said, "Where have you been?" As if she was the one who'd been hiding from an ex-girlfriend cop, had the body of an ex-con friend incinerated, and planned a ransom score with the nephew of a local boxer. The same nephew who happened to be Sam's ex-boyfriend.

"I've been studying," she said.

"Oh," George looked out toward the lake as a half dozen Canada Geese took off into the air. "I would've stopped by the diner to say hello, but I wasn't sure if your uncle'd have his shotgun ready for me."

Sam glanced down toward the ground and shook her head. "He wouldn't do that." She pushed a strand of hair back from her face and tucked it behind her ear. "I finished my exams this morning," she said, as if she wanted to change the subject.

"Cool," George said. "You do okay?"

She shrugged. "I hope so."

George looked off again. "Are you almost done with your run? Maybe we can grab a coffee?"

She shook her head. "I'd like to get in a few more laps. But then I'm meeting some friends."

"Oh, okay."

They both stood quiet, with an awkward feeling stuck in the air.

"Are you working tonight?" he said.

Sam shook her head. "I took a few days off from

the diner, while I had my exams. Told my uncle I needed some time to myself."

"You want to meet later? Maybe get a drink?"

She smiled. "There's a good band playing near my apartment, maybe we could do that?"

George thought for a moment. "I can pick you up?"

Sam looked down at the bike between his legs. "Can you fit two people on this?" She laughed and pulled her phone from her back pocket. "Why don't you give me your number, and I'll call you."

George remembered he left his phone in Louie's car. He looked down toward the ground. "I don't have my phone."

"That's okay. Just give me your number, and—"

"No, it's just... I don't know the number. I've only had the phone for a few days. I know that sounds weird, but..." He thought for a moment. "How about I give you my sister's number?"

She shrugged and he gave her Joyce's number. She tapped it into her phone, then stared back at him for a moment. "I don't know if I need to call. You can just meet me there. It's a place called The Fuzzy Grape. Or you can come by my apartment... it's a five minute walk."

"You can give me your address. I should be able to remember it. Plan B is I'll meet you at the Fuzzy Grape."

She gave him her address. "Nine o'clock?"

34

LOUIE AND NICK sat together on the couch out on the three-season porch, facing the TV when George walked in.

Louie turned and looked back at George over his shoulder. "Where the hell've you been?"

"I had to meet someone."

"Meet who? You said you'd meet me back here over an hour ago."

George glanced at Nick and the two exchanged a look. "You worried about me?"

Louie nodded. "Yeah, worried you get pinched, they're coming after me." Louie stuck an unlit cigarette in his mouth. "We decided you should call Victor."

"*Me?*" George said. "Why *me?*"

Louie shrugged. "Obviously, the kid's not gonna call his own uncle about his own kidnapping, ask for ransom..."

George shook his head as he looked back at Louie. "Why don't you call?"

"He might recognize my voice. I've talked to him before at the bar. But you... you've never said a word to him, have you?"

George made a face. "When have you talked to him? He doesn't have any *idea* who you are."

"I talked to him at Keenan's. More than once."

George sighed. "Jesus, Louie. Then change your voice."

"What, you afraid to make the call?" Louie said.

"I'm not afraid at all. It's just..."

Nick got up from the couch. "Shit, you two are unbelievable. You're like an old married couple." Nick walked past them, through the doorway, and into the kitchen.

George turned to Louie. "Where the hell's he going? You ask me, he's gotten himself a little too comfortable around here, don't you think?" He looked back toward the doorway. "Where's Joyce?"

Louie said, "She's at work."

"She went to work?"

Nick walked back into the room with a can of 7-Up in his hand. He sat back down on the couch and grabbed the TV remote off the coffee table.

George turned, watched Nick for a moment. "What about him? Have him call his uncle, cry for help. We let *him* deliver the message."

Nick turned and looked up at George from the

couch. "I can't call. He'll read right through it. Probably tell me to call my other uncle." He sipped his 7-Up. "Besides, I'm just a poor, helpless kid. That's what you keep calling me, isn't it? *Kid this, kid that.* I'm almost twenty-six, you know."

"Don't be so goddamn sensitive." Louie rolled his eyes and shook his head. "George is right. It makes sense... you make the call."

Nick let out a slight laugh, looked back and forth from Louie to George. "You're not very good at any of this, are you. What's the deal, was the dead guy the one in charge? You can't even make a decision."

"Shut your goddamn mouth, kid." Louie stepped closer to the couch, his finger pointed toward Nick's face.

"I'm just saying, who cares who calls? You really think he's going to know your voice? Either of you? Just call him, tell him you're going to kill me if he doesn't pay up a couple grand... meet him somewhere and we make the exchange." Nick clapped his hands together. "Done deal... no?"

George closed his eyes for a moment, took a deep breath as he imagined this going down the wrong road. Not that it'd ever gone in the direction he'd expected. Not with Earl around from the beginning —the instigator—getting people to do what he wanted.

And now he wasn't around to fix the mess.

Louie looked at his watch. "Let's call now, give him

a few hours to get the money."

"A few hours? Don't you think he'd need more time?" George said. "I was thinking tomorrow would make more sense." George thought about Sam, wondered how he'd even get over to her house now that Joyce wasn't around—not that she'd be too excited to let him use her car.

Louie said, "No, we do it tonight. And maybe we tell him, throw in the belt. Make another threat, his girlfriend or something."

Nick stood up from the couch. "He won't do it. He'd give up his own mother before he'd give up that belt."

Louie looked at George and shrugged, half a smile on his face. "Then we grab the mother."

Nick shook his head and sat back down on the couch. "Actually, my grandmother's dead."

Louie pulled a piece of paper from his jeans, handed it to George. "Here's the number. It's his cell." Louie walked out of the room toward the kitchen, came right back in with the plastic 7-Eleven bag and pulled out one of the flip phones. He handed it to George. "Just change your voice, if you're that worried about it." He walked over to the wet bar and grabbed a rag, threw it to George. "Put this over the mouthpiece."

George stood quiet with the phone in one hand, the rag and the piece of paper with Victor's phone number in the other. He looked down at the paper

then back at Louie. "Is this a three or an eight?"

Louie took the paper from his hand. "Where? There's no three on here."

George leaned over and pointed to the number. "That's a *two*," Louie said.

George shook his head. "No, here."

Louie pulled the paper in closer and squinted his eyes. "Oh, yeah. That's an eight."

George shook his head. "Why are we doing it like this? Can't we at least write-out some kind of a plan? We haven't even talked about what I'm supposed to say."

George glanced at Nick, saw him roll his eyes.

Louie said, "What, you want to leave a nice paper trail with all our notes? Just to make sure the prosecution can take us down?"

George took a deep breath, looked out toward the yard through the screens. "We haven't even discussed where we're meeting him."

"Tell him at a park or something. Roger Williams. Or a school... one of the high schools." Louie shrugged. "Improvise."

Nick laughed. "Holy shit, you two really *are* unbelievable."

Louie pulled his gun from his pants and pointed it at Nick. "I'm telling you right now, kid, one more word out of you and I swear I'll..."

"Put that thing away," George said. "We already owe Sal twenty-five grand."

"Dial the phone," Louie said with a nod toward George. "Tell him, meet us at eight o'clock tonight and he gets his nephew back. Any later, the kid dies. And tell him we'll make sure everyone knows it was his fault."

George looked at the clock under the TV. He thought about Sam, and wasn't going to miss meeting her at nine. The last thing he wanted to do was blow it. He knew it was his last chance. "If it's tonight, then it's got to be later. One, maybe two in the morning."

Louie gave George a look. "You got a date or something? You want us to sit around, wait for you until you're good and ready?"

George stared back at Louie. "You know what? I don't need to do this. You want to see what you can bleed Victor for, you go ahead." He walked out the doorway and into the kitchen. He grabbed a can of beer from the refrigerator and walked back onto the porch. "You know, I wish I'd never come back here. I should've gotten away from all this bullshit when I had the chance."

"Oh, here we go," Louie said. "What are you going to do, go out to Hollywood? Wander around, try to figure out what you're going to be when you grow up?" He laughed. "Jesus, George, you're like dealing with a little boy."

Nick stood up from the couch. "This is a disaster," he said. "Maybe this isn't such a good idea."

Louie pulled his Glock from his pants and moved it back and forth from George to Nick. He stopped and held it on Nick. "Sit your ass back down on that couch. We're doing this tonight. And I'll tell you what... I'm getting that goddamn championship belt, too."

George couldn't believe what he was seeing. "What are you going to do, shoot us?"

Louie tucked the gun back in his pants and walked toward the wet bar. He poured himself a Jim Beam, took a sip and walked to the tall pub table in the corner of the room. He sat on one of the stools, looked down into his glass then shot the whole thing back, finished every last drop. With his eyes on George, he said, "Give me the goddamn phone."

George stepped toward him and put the phone down on the table. He ripped the towel from George's hand. George put the paper with Victor's number down in front of him.

Louie held the paper up in front of him, squinted his eyes and dialed the phone.

Nick walked over and stood next to George and Louie at the table. They watched Louie as he held the cloth over the lower half of the phone, where the mic was. He held the phone up to his ear.

"This Victor?" he said. He paused. "Nevermind who this is. Shut your mouth for a second and listen. We have your nephew." Louie looked at Nick. "Nick." He listened. "Yes, your nephew Nick. We have him hostage. And unless you want his blood on your hands, you get two-hundred-fifty grand ready by midnight tonight. And that championship belt of yours... I want that too. You don't show up, you don't have the money... he's dead." Louie nodded, confident as he listened to Victor. "You tell anyone we called... he's dead. You pull any shit, he's dead. You understand?" Louie paused a moment, his eyes narrowed, his head tilted a bit with the phone up against his ear. "What do you mean you don't have any money? Then you get it."

Nick's eyebrows were high up on his head as he watched Louie. His mouth hung a bit open.

George walked over to the wet bar and poured himself a drink. He walked back over to the table with Nick and Louie.

Louie spoke into the phone. "I'm not giving you time. You get it tonight, by midnight. Answer this phone at eleven o'clock, I'll give you the location."

George couldn't believe what he was hearing.

Louie said, "What do you mean, *why am I calling you?* Aren't you the uncle?"

George and Nick exchanged a look.

"No, this isn't a friggin joke, Victor." Louie shook his head. "Get the money and the belt. Expect my call at eleven." Louie pressed the button on the phone and ended the call.

"What'd he say?" Nick said as he watched Louie walk to the wet bar with his empty glass.

Louie said, "What a prick that guy is. Told me to call one of his other relatives."

George said, "Is he going to meet us?"

Louie didn't answer as he poured himself another bourbon and took a sip. "Let's hope so."

35

GEORGE HAD JUST gotten out of the shower, drying his hair with a towel when Joyce walked in the front door. Nick was in the kitchen boiling pasta.

"Why don't you make yourself right at home," she said with a touch of attitude that normally came from her voice.

Nick turned to her. "Jesus, sorry. I thought I'd make something to eat. I didn't think—"

"I'm not talking to you," she said to Nick as she put her backpack down on the chair at the kitchen table. She turned and looked at George as he stood in the doorway in jeans, but no shirt. "Christ, get dressed, will you?"

"What is it with you two?" Nick said. "The way you treat each other. All three of you, actually."

"Shut your mouth, Nick," Joyce said. "You don't know him... what he put me and my mother through all these years. It gets old, you know."

George used his hands to brush back his wet hair, the towel hung around his neck. "I took a shower. Does that really bother you?"

"Just put a damn shirt on," she said.

Nick said, "You got any sauce? For the spaghetti?"

Joyce nodded toward the refrigerator. "In the freezer, hon. In the Tupperware container with the blue top."

George turned and walked back toward the bathroom.

He grabbed his Sperrys and threw a shirt on he'd found in the closet in the hall. It was a little tight, but it's all he had. There was no time to get out to Louie's for his clothes.

He walked back out into the kitchen. "Joyce, Mind if I ask a favor?"

She had a beer in her hand, cracked the top and took a sip. "Depends."

George hesitated a moment. "Can I use your car?"

Joyce let out a slight snort. "You're serious?"

"Just for a few hours. I'll fill it up with—"

"No," she said. "You can't. I need it."

"Come on. I'll get out of here... you and Nick can have the place to yourselves."

"Oh, thank you for giving me permission to have my own house to myself. *How nice of you.*"

"I'm just saying, I'll be out of your hair."

She sipped her beer and looked past George toward the window at the front of the house. She glanced back at him. "Where're you going?"

"To meet someone."

Nick said, "My uncle?"

George shook his head. "No. That's later."

"I'll drop you off," Joyce said. "Maybe your friend's mommy can drive you home?" Joyce laughed —somewhat of a cackle—and finished off her can of beer. "Where's Louie? Use *his* car."

"Can't. Not tonight," George said.

Nick turned from the stove. "Louie's out getting supplies."

"Supplies for what?"

"To meet Nick's uncle."

Joyce looked Nick up and down as she bit her lower lip. "Does that mean I won't see you around here anymore?"

George rolled his eyes. "Joyce, you're going to make me sick."

"I'm just asking a question." She held out her hand toward Nick. "See, he even cooks."

George said to Joyce, "You get a cut, too, you know. We split it four ways. I'm giving Roy some of my cut... for helping clean up the mess back at Louie's."

"How many times do I have to tell you, I don't want to be involved in your criminal activity."

"It's a couple hundred grand. Plus the belt might be worth another two hundred."

Joyce widened her eyes. "Two hundred?"

George nodded. "Thousand."

"I thought you said it wasn't worth shit?"

"Not the belt we have now. I'm talking about the one Nick's uncle still has in his house."

Nick lifted the pot of pasta over to the sink and dumped it into the colander. He turned his head as the steam shot up toward his face. "My uncle claims his belt is worth a quarter-million." He shook his head. "But I won't be surprised if he chooses the belt over me."

"He wouldn't give it up for his own nephew?" Joyce said.

Nick shrugged as he poured the pasta into a large bowl.

Joyce turned to George. "You need a ride, like I said, I'll drop you off."

"Someone needs to stay with Nick," George said.

Nick stirred the sauce in with the pasta. He looked at George and narrowed his eyes. "You still don't trust me?"

"About as much as my own sister trusts me."

Joyce gave Nick a look. "That's not much."

George brushed his hand through the air, toward Joyce. He walked out the door. "Forget it, I'll take my bike."

Nick said, "You don't want to eat?"

George didn't look back, slammed the door closed behind him and walked around the side of the garage. He grabbed his bike and jumped on the seat as he got a running start, then peddled hard into the street.

By the time he rode all the way to the back parking lot of JJ's Furniture Warehouse, it was already close to nine. He wished he'd gotten Samantha's number so could at least let her know he'd have to meet her at the show. He'd leave out the part he was going to steal back the Toyota Louie'd left in the parking lot.

He got off his bike and walked it toward the car. It was still parked right where they left it. He didn't know if it was a good idea to drive the thing, even wondered if Earl was lying when he said the plates were clean.

George leaned his bike down on the ground and got down on his knees. He stuck his head under the car and saw the keys Louie had tossed underneath. He was surprised they were still there.

He didn't want to get down on the ground and get his shirt dirty before he met Sam. But he didn't have much of a choice. He got down on his stomach, slid himself under the car, and reached his hand as far as he could. But his fingers couldn't reach the keys. Not unless he got himself right under the car, which he'd hoped to avoid.

He walked over toward a wooded area at the backside of the lot, looked on the ground and found a long stick. He went back and tried again. He reached the keys without a problem.

He removed the front wheel from his bike, popped the lid and fit the bike in the trunk. As he slammed down the lid something caught his attention.

A police vehicle pulled into the lot.

"Shit," he said under his breath as he turned and looked all around the area in somewhat of a panic, not sure if he should run for the woods or duck inside the car.

He did neither and instead stuck his hands in his pants' pockets and strolled toward the entrance to JJ's Furniture Warehouse. He whistled, tried to stay calm as he acted like any other customer going to check out the cheap furniture.

He got to the door and glanced over his shoulder.

The cop was gone. So instead of going inside, he turned and headed back for the Toyota.

His phone rang. It was Louie.

As soon as George answered, Louie said, "Where the hell are you?"

George hesitated a moment. "You don't want to know."

"Actually, I *do* want to know. Otherwise I wouldn't have asked."

George rolled his eyes and sighed into the phone. "Okay, what's up?"

"What's up? I'm at Joyce's house looking for you,

that's what's up. She thinks you're out on a date. I hope she's wrong."

With the phone in his ear, George walked around to the back of JJ's Warehouse toward the Toyota. "Joyce is nuts, as if you don't know that already. I never told her where I was going. I never said anything about a date." He looked up from the phone and again spotted the police vehicle. It drove slow between the rows of cars in the lot.

"She said you were all cleaned up. She's sure you're out on some kind of a date."

George watched the police vehicle. "Louie, I gotta run. Let me call you back."

"Why the hell would you be out, doing who knows what, when we're meeting Victor at—"

"I'll call you back." George hung up without letting Louie finish. He walked back to the entrance to JJ's and up to the sliding glass doors.

"George?"

He turned when he heard his name.

Dawn was alone in her car, the passenger window down she leaned across the seat and looked right at George. "Buying some furniture?" she said. "With your bike?"

George stepped toward the edge of the sidewalk in front of the building. "My bike?"

She nodded. "I saw you riding it, back there a couple of miles ago. Long ride to come look at cheap furniture."

George stared back at her for a moment, stepped toward the car and leaned on the open window on the passenger side.

Dawn straightened up in the driver's seat.

George said, "Wasn't once enough for you?"

She looked back at him with a confused look on her face.

He said, "I spent three years in the can. I have you to thank for that."

"You have me to thank?" She shook her head as she turned to him, her elbow up on the steering wheel and the other arm on the back of her seat. "You blame me? Like I'm the one who decided to go down the road you chose?"

"I did my time. I hoped maybe we could put it all behind us. I thought maybe you'd stop trying to take me down again, whether I'm guilty of something or not."

"Are you?"

George backed away from her car. "Do you have something on me? Then go ahead and arrest me. If not, then I think it's time we let this go, once and for all."

Dawn didn't say a word but stared back at him.

He turned and started to walk away from her car and only made it as far as the sliding doors when Dawn said, "George? Can you tell me why you put your bike in the trunk of that Toyota?"

36

GEORGE SAT ON the cold, metal bench in the holding cell at the Providence County Police station. With his elbows on his knees, his head hung down with his face in his hands. He lifted his eyes as Dawn pulled a key from her belt and unlocked the cell.

She slid open the steel-barred door and gave George a nod with her chin. "You're free to go."

George stood from the bench and stared at Dawn. "Really?"

She led him by the arm down the hall, through a solid door with a single, small pane of glass and out into the lobby. She held the door as George walked past her.

Frank sat in one of the chairs along the wall.

"Frank?" George said.

Dawn pulled George toward the window at the counter.

The cop behind the glass slid a large, yellow

envelope toward George through the opening under the window.

George opened it, pulled out his wallet and his Casio watch. He opened the wallet and looked inside before he slipped it in his back pocket. He took the key to Louie's apartment from the envelope and put it in his front pocket. He turned to Frank. "Did you pay my bail?"

Dawn stood behind George. "There aren't any charges being filed." She gave Frank a nod and shook his hand. "Thanks for coming to get him. I would've given him a ride, but..." She turned to George. "The car's not been reported stolen, with no record of a registration. I do have to give you a written warning for driving an unregistered vehicle." She gave him a smile, turned and walked back through the same door they just walked out of.

George stayed quiet as Frank kept his eyes on the road, driving five miles-an-hour under the speed limit in his Corvette. Without turning to George, he said, "She's a good person. She didn't have to call me, you know. And I'm sure she did what she could to get you out of whatever trouble you got into."

George watched Frank for a moment, then turned toward the passenger window. "I'm sorry you had to come out like this... in the middle of the night."

Frank shrugged. "To me, it's morning. I get up in another hour anyway."

"I called Louie with my one phone call. He didn't answer."

Frank turned and looked right at George. "They didn't tell you?"

"They didn't tell me *what?*"

Frank turned the wheel, jumped onto 95 heading west. It took him a couple of moments to continue. "I don't want you to tell me what you were involved in. I don't care if you were or not, but—"

"Frank, what happened?"

"You know Victor Albanese, right?"

George stared back at him, waiting...

Frank glanced at George. "You really have no idea what I'm talking about?"

George shook his head. "Frank, Jesus... spit it out, will you?"

"Louie was shot. Apparently he—"

"Louie? He got shot? Holy *shit.* Is he all right?"

Frank nodded. "I think so. At least as far as I know. Apparently he had Victor's nephew... demanded Victor give him money in exchange for the kid." He shrugged. "I don't know, I guess Louie wanted ransom. To be honest, the story was a little confusing."

George's heart pounded in his chest. "Who told you? Where'd you hear this?"

"I stopped at Keenan's. It's all they were talking

about. It was on the news."

George stared straight ahead toward the highway. "He's not dead? Are you sure?"

Frank shook his head. "They said Victor had the works at the scene where Louie told him to meet. It was behind one of the schools. State cops were there, had men up on the roof from what they're saying."

"Why wouldn't Dawn've said something? She had to've known." George swallowed hard. His mind raced. "What about the nephew?"

"Name's Nick. Used to be a boxer, like his uncle." Frank paused a moment. "Heard he wasn't any good."

The two drove quiet for a couple of miles until Frank said, "Where am I dropping you off? Your sister's? I can put you up on a couch at my place if you want."

Each breath George took was heavy. His heart pounded so hard he could hear it in his ears. Frank spoke but his voice faded into George's own thoughts. He didn't know what to do. Maybe ask Frank to take him to the train station? Get out of there once and for all? He wondered if maybe Nick had set the whole thing up, lied about his relationship with Victor. Obviously Victor called the cops when Louie told him not to. Either he didn't care what happened to Nick or he knew he'd be all right.

"George?" Frank said. "Where we going?"

George hesitated for a moment, then gave Frank an address, told him to drop him off at Samantha's apartment.

The rain was coming down hard when Frank pulled up in front of Samantha's apartment. "You want me to wait?"

George stepped out of his car then leaned into the passenger side and shook his head. "No, I'll be all right." As he started to close the door he turned back again. "I can't say for sure I'll be around much anymore, Frank. I don't know if you got someone else to work in the back or..."

Frank brushed his hand toward George. "You don't need to be working in the back of a pizza place, George. I'm sure there's something out there for you. Something legal, I'd hope." He gave George a nod and a tight smile. "You're a smart kid, George. I hope you find a way to do the right thing."

George stood still for a moment then closed the car door. He walked toward Samantha's building and glanced back over his shoulder as Frank pulled away from the curb. He watched until Frank's car disappeared around the corner. Under his breath, George said, "Thanks, Frank."

He looked up and down the building, pretty sure this was the right place. He rang the third doorbell on top, then stepped back and looked up toward the windows on the third floor. It was dark inside, other than what looked like light from a lamp.

He rang the doorbell again and stepped back as he kept his eyes up toward the top-floor.

Shadows moved behind the windows. He hoped it was Samantha. Not that she'd be happy he never showed up. It's not like he'd tell her he spent the night in jail.

The light went on behind the door. George tried to see in through the sheer curtains hanging over the inside of the window. He saw feet—slippers—come down the stairs and he stepped back from the door.

One latch clicked followed by another as the door opened and a young woman—younger than George, anyway—stood in the doorway in sweatpants and a baggy sweatshirt.

"Can I help you?" she said.

"Uh, sorry. I thought this was—" He looked up at the building number over the door. "I'm looking for Samantha. This is her apartment, I hope?"

She nodded. "It is. It was." She folded her arms at her chest. "You're looking for Samantha? At five-thirty in the morning?" She narrowed her eyes. "Are you *George*, by any chance?"

George nodded. "Is she here?"

She shook her head. "No."

"No? Is she—"

"She told me not to tell you where she went if you

ever showed up. She waited for you..." She shrugged. "You're a little late."

"Please, I have to talk to her. Can you just tell me where she is?"

The young woman stared back at him, waiting a couple of moments. She said, "She took the train back home."

"Home? You mean—"

"Florida. She may be back for graduation but..." She shook her head and smiled with a thin line between her lips. "Sorry."

"So she left? Just like that?"

The woman let out a slight snort. "She said you were smart. But you're having a hard time getting what I said through your head."

George looked at his watch, held his wrist under the dim light over the door. "What time did she leave?"

"I dropped her off. A little more than an hour ago. She didn't want me to tell you."

George turned and looked out toward the wet, slick street in front of him as the rain came down on his head. He turned back to the woman, watching him from the doorway.

She stared back at George without saying a word and shook her head.

"I want to call her. Please, can you—"

She had started to close the door but stuck her head out through the opening. "A little past the point of exchanging phone numbers, don't you think?"

37

GEORGE MADE THE long walk to Joyce's house in a little under two hours. He took his time as the heavy rain poured over him. Her car was in the driveway but there were no lights on inside. He didn't think she'd be asleep, not unless for some reason she had no idea what had happened to Louie.

He tried the knob on the front door, but it was locked. He pressed his face against the glass pane and looked inside, saw beer bottles on the counter and an empty bottle of Jim Beam on the table.

He knocked and within a couple of seconds Joyce opened the door.

"Where the hell have you been?" she said. She had that growl she always had in her voice. "That son-of-a-bitch turned on Louie, told his uncle everything."

"I told you we couldn't trust him," George said.

Joyce squinted her eyes. "There you go again. It's everyone else's fault, right?" She walked in from the doorway. "Where'd you go? Out on a date while your ex brother-in-law was getting locked up?"

"I was in jail." George closed the door behind him and walked past Joyce. "Why are all the lights off?"

"What do you mean *you* were in jail?"

"I went back to get that Toyota at JJ's Furniture Warehouse. I told you. I needed a car."

Joyce turned and looked through the window at the street, then walked from the kitchen and out to the screened-in porch. "I told Louie to wait for you," she said. "But he thought you'd changed your mind and bailed on him." She sat down on the couch and turned the television on with the remote in her hand. "You're far from a perfect man, George. But like I told Louie, you'd never bail on your friends."

George pulled a chair from against the wall and started to sit.

"What are you doing?" Joyce said. "Go dry yourself off if you're going to sit down."

George stood and looked down at his wet clothes clinging to his damp skin. "It's just water." He walked toward the back of the porch and looked out through the screen door into the yard. It was still dark but the rain had stopped.

With his back to Joyce, he said, "So what else have you heard?"

"Not much. Sounds like his bail will be set in the morning." She shook her head and looked off. "It's not good, George. And I don't have the money to help him."

George turned from the screen door. "Where's the belt?"

She pointed with her thumb toward the garage on the other side of the wall. "Louie put it in the garage, up in the rafters."

"Maybe I should go see what it's worth. Go talk to one of Louie's friends."

Joyce didn't respond. "Did you see the note I left?"

"What *note*?"

She nodded with her chin in the direction of the doorway. "Someone called looking for you."

George started toward the kitchen. "Who was it?"

She brushed the back of her hand through the air. "I don't know. Go read the note."

He stood in the middle of the kitchen for a moment and looked around. He didn't see any notes or even a piece of paper. "Where is it?" he yelled.

"By the phone."

He looked along the counter. He lifted the base of the phone and looked down on the floor. A piece of paper sticking out from under the refrigerator caught his eye. He bent down to pick it up. It had Samantha's name written on it with a phone number he could barely make out scratched underneath. He walked back out to the room and looked at Joyce from the doorway. "When did she call?"

"Who?"

"Sam."

Joyce turned and looked at George over the back of the couch. "I look like your goddamn secretary?"

"You can't just tell me?"

Joyce let out a sigh and turned back to the television. "I have no idea what time it was. You were in the shower."

George's eyes opened wide. He pushed his wet hair back on his head and left his hand, holding it back there for a moment. "I was in the *shower*? I was *here* when she called? And you didn't tell me?"

She shrugged. "I did. I left a note. With all the whining you were doing before you left..."

George stared at the back of her head and closed his eyes for a moment. He looked down at the note, then turned from the doorway and went back into the kitchen. He picked up the phone and dialed the number.

But it didn't even ring once. His call went right to voicemail.

He listened to her voice, and for a moment almost smiled. But after the beep he started his rambling message. "Sam, hey... uh... it's George. I'm sorry. I mean, I'm sorry I didn't show up tonight. Something bad happened. Not bad, but... actually it was pretty bad. But... I'm sorry. I went to your apartment. I guess you're already gone, but... I don't know if you talked to your roommate already. I..." He stopped before another word came out when he saw headlights shine in through the windows from outside. "Oh shit," he said under his breath.

He hung up the phone and turned from the window, knocked over a kitchen chair and ran through the doorway into the other room. "Joyce! The cops! They're outside!"

Joyce stood from the couch and looked at George but he didn't say another word and ran past her. He crashed through the screen door at the back of the porch and jumped down the steps and across the grass.

He moved as fast as he could straight into the woods and didn't look back until he ended up in someone's backyard. He ran out to the street and stopped, looked both ways, then ran into the morning darkness for as far as he could go.

He kept running until he couldn't continue anymore and collapsed on the side of the road. He crawled on his hands and knees up into the dark, wet woods and leaned his back against a tree. His legs were bent in front of him and his arms hung over his knees. He tried to slow his breathing. He had a hard time catching his breath. He still had the note in his hand and held it up in front of him, then closed his eyes.

He knew he had to keep going and leaned against the tree to push himself up onto his feet. He took a deep breath, then took off without another thought and ran as fast as his legs would let him.

It took a good two hours until he made it to the highway. He walked along Route 10 then onto Route 6 just outside downtown. He stayed up in the tall grass on the hill and climbed the wall up to Dean Street, followed it down past the Providence Journal building on Fountain Street. He was careful and tried to stay out from under the street lamps, although the sun was already starting to come up.

He turned onto Gaspee Street and picked up his pace until he stopped under the tree canopy across from the Amtrak Station. His feet were heavier than they'd ever been. He looked down at a park bench, but knew he couldn't sit.

He looked around before he crossed Gaspee and headed into the train station.

The only other person inside was a man in a blue Amtrak hat behind the service window.

The man looked up when George walked in.

George was hungry and wet and tired and knew he wasn't thinking straight.

But he was already there.

He walked to the window and stopped before he got to the man. He looked up at the schedule and studied it for a moment, then reached into his pocket and pulled out a wet wad of bills. He stepped toward the window and put the money down on the counter.

The man looked at the cash then looked at George

and held his gaze for a moment. "Can I help you, son?"

George swallowed and nodded then leaned down and put his face close to the glass at the opening at the bottom of the window. "Yes, sir." He still hadn't completely caught his breath. "How much for a one-way ticket to Florida?"

If you enjoyed *Drag the Man Down*, please share your thoughts with others by leaving a review with the online store where you purchased it. (Find your store's link). It would mean a lot to me as an author and to others interested in learning what readers like you think about the book. Thank you!

Please Join My Reader List

I'd like to invite you to join my reader list to receive free stories, giveaways, and VIP announcements when my new books are released. When you do, you'll receive two free books, *Tell Them I'm Dead* and *What Have You Done?*.

Visit **GregoryPayette.com/free-book** to sign up now.

Other Books by Gregory Payette

The Henry Walsh Private Investigator Series

Henry Walsh Series Book 1: Dead at Third

Henry Walsh Series Book 2: The Last Ride

Henry Walsh Series Book 3: The Crystal Pelican

Henry Walsh Series Book 4: The Night the Music
Died

Henry Walsh Series Book 5: Dead Men Don't Smile

Henry Walsh Series Book 6: Dead in the Creek

~

Standalones and Short Stories

Tell Them I'm Dead

What Have You Done?

Half Cocked

Danny Womack's .38

Learn more by visiting **GregoryPayette.com**

www.ingramcontent.com/pod-product-compliance
Lightning Source LLC
Chambersburg PA
CBHW020248030426
42336CB00010B/669